The Mind Games THEY Play

11 Proven Strategies to Identify, Understand, and Resist Manipulation and Master the Art of Human Psychology.

HALBERT WARD

TABLE OF CONTENTS

INTRODUCTION

Reading a person's mind is a skill that anybody can learn. Anybody can play mind games. You can know what your client needs even before they open their mouth to say anything or you can know the best way to approach your boss to get a favorable outcome. When you develop an intuition about the things that others find valuable, it will help you move further in life.

Perceptive people often enjoy more success in their personal lives and professional lives. Individuals who perform excellently well are not always the smartest individuals; they are the individuals who form a good connection with other people and possess a higher emotional quotient.

People are always sending signals about what they are thinking about. Although they are sending these signals all the time, practice is required to tune in. When the messages you are getting from an individual are saying that you and the individual are not on the same page, the clues you are getting are telling you to take a step back and then redirect. They are saying you should change the conversation to something else or change the way you are approaching the conversation. There are a variety of ways you can read people's minds or guess what is on their minds and then develop better personal and business relationships.

In this book, we discuss the interesting world of mind control and equip you with the necessary tools and strategies you need to develop healthy relationships with people and protect yourself from manipulation.

So, what is mind control, and how can you control a person's mind?

The subject of mind control is a captivating and even concerning one that people have been curious about for ages. Whether you want to understand what is actually happening in toxic relationships or you want to explore the manipulative tactics that leaders of cults usually use, learning about mind control is important for your emotional and mental well-being.

When you understand mind control's principles, you get better equipped to recognize when you are being manipulated and you are able to resist its influence. Having this knowledge empowers you and makes you able to make informed decisions that will help you in your life, develop healthy relationships that are based on respect and trust, and you are able to assert your boundaries.

The purpose of this book is to help you understand how mind control works so that you can use it to improve your life and protect yourself from manipulators who want to use it against you. The book is not about teaching you how to control the minds of people for unethical purposes.

We will discuss the factors that are responsible for manipulation, symptoms to look out for, and practical strategies you can use to break free from the manipulator's grip. You will learn to form healthy relationship dynamics and your dating experiences will be enhanced.

The process of getting a person to change their mind involves taking into account the person's beliefs, life experience, education, and values. This will help you know the right approach to take. Since everything is reliant upon the willingness of the individual to accept an idea that is new, continuously providing more and more data because you want to back up your claim might cause them to resist all evidence and discard it. Therefore, instead of making them feel intimidated, you can make them feel comfortable as it will open them to suggestions.

You might attempt to change a person's core values. It is often impossible to prove an individual's belief system wrong. However, you can make them experience reality differently, and this can make them change the core beliefs that they have. When a person witnesses a moment like this without any external influence, there is a belief by the subject that they are questioning reality objectively. The influence this has on them is stronger than if a person told them to question an idea coming from someone else.

Making an individual change their mind and do what you want them to do does not have to be complicated. If you master the art of human psychology, you can use it to influence individuals by making the right appeals that they will comply with. You can change the minds of people by following steps that work subconsciously on them.

Is there any individual that you have struggled to persuade previously? After reading this book, you will be able to easily persuade them. You will develop the skills needed to face less resistance to your ideas and people will be more receptive to changing their minds.

This book will give you deeper insights on manipulation, and you will be able to find out if there is any manipulator in your life.

Any relationship can become abusive or emotionally manipulative even though manipulation is mostly talked about in romantic relationships' context. Relationships with manipulators may include relationships with abusive or toxic parents, overbearing or narcissistic partners, bosses, neighbors, roommates, friends, or in-laws. While you will likely not be emotionally manipulated in all of these areas we have mentioned, it is important that you know the common signs of manipulation and learn how to respond to it if you find yourself in such a situation.

The eleven chapters of this book reveal 11 strategies that can help you identify and understand manipulation. You will learn how to resist manipulation and use psychology to improve your life. Let us dive into the first chapter.

CHAPTER ONE:
Understanding Manipulation

Manipulation is a type of emotional abuse that is used to influence, control, and exploit other individuals to one's advantage. Manipulation controls how a person thinks, feels, and behaves in order for the manipulative individual to achieve their aim.

It is natural for individuals in relationships to encounter problems as the relationship continues to grow. Sometimes, greed or emotions can cause these issues. Manipulation is one problem that can come up in any kind of relationship. You need to know the signs of manipulation and how to handle it when it surfaces in your relationships.

Manipulation can occur in casual or close relationships, but you will find manipulation more in relationships that are closely formed. It includes any attempt that someone makes to sway another person's emotions to make them feel or act a certain way. It involves the exercise of influence over other people. Individuals who manipulate other people attack their emotional and mental sides to achieve their desires. The person who is manipulating others, and who is known as the manipulator, does so to create a power imbalance. The manipulator takes advantage of you to get privileges, control, power, and benefits. Manipulators use some common tricks to make you feel irrational and then increase the likelihood of having you do what they want you to do.

Although people display manipulative behavior every day, exhibiting a pattern of the tactics of manipulation is a sign of abuse. This may mean that the abuser has a serious mental health disorder, such as antisocial personality disorder or narcissistic personality disorder.

Are You Being Manipulated?

Many manipulative individuals are highly skilled at getting you to believe that they are not doing anything that is wrong. If you suspect that you are being manipulated, what you should do is think about how that individual makes you feel after you interact with them.

One sign you can check for is if you are having feelings of confusion. When a person has pure, loving, and good intentions towards you, you will rarely be confused. Another sign to check for is if you feel fearful or hesitant to speak about your feelings openly or address your confusion. It is a red flag if you find it difficult to express your needs or ask a question without it turning into an argument. When an individual is defensive, it could be a sign that the person is feeling caught.

Tactics Used in Manipulation

Manipulation tactics, also known as psychological or emotional manipulation tactics, give the manipulative individual a sense of control and power. Manipulation also ensures that the needs of the manipulative individual are met. A relationship is toxic if it has a pattern of manipulation tactics that is consistent. This pattern could also be a sign that a person is in a psychologically/emotionally abusive relationship.

Tactics of manipulation are the particular ways that an individual who is emotionally abusive attacks their victims. The individual uses the tactics to control their victim by eroding the victim's self-confidence and making them dependent on the abuser, thereby making it hard to leave the relationship. Common manipulation tactics include seeking control and gaslighting, but an abuser can control their victims through the use of many other tactics. You can use therapy to heal from trauma.

Manipulation can occur in a variety of forms. In fact, when someone behaves in a kind manner, they may be manipulating you, depending on what they hope to achieve.

Manipulators have common traits. These traits include:
- They make you depend more on them by convincing you to give up an important thing.
- They are experts at using your insecurities against you.
- They are aware of the weaknesses you have and they know how to exploit those weaknesses.
- They don't stop manipulating you. They continue until you get yourself out of the situation.

There are a variety of tactics that people use to manipulate others. Some other manipulation signs include:

Endlessly judging you.
The manipulative individual does not mask their manipulation behind good fun or humor. In this situation, they go the route of ridiculing, judging, and dismissing you. They do their best to make you feel like what you are doing is wrong, and that you will never be good enough for them no matter what you do. The manipulator only focuses on negativity and never provides any constructive solutions.

Denial and lying.
Manipulative individuals may tell their victims lies. After bombarding them with lies and they are caught, they may cover up with more lies or deny the lies.

Intensifying insecurities.
Sadly, emotional manipulators are experts at noticing the insecurities of a person and intensifying them. The manipulator targets an individual's sense of shame, which is a feeling of inadequacy within the individual. Since shame is an emotion that is painful that many individuals avoid, triggering their shame encourages them to do what the manipulator wants so that they can avoid feeling it in the future.

The manipulator is an expert at playing on an individual's insecurities. They use this tactic to attack your weaknesses and increase your feelings of insecurity. They feel like they are psychologically superior when they make you look bad. The manipulator uses the tactic of knowing your sensitivities or unique triggers and uses them against you. Some individuals are experts at studying people and knowing the exact buttons to press to manipulate them. For instance, if you had a self-absorbed or selfish parent as a child and you didn't feel important because they were accusing you of being selfish, it would be a tactic that manipulators can use. The manipulator can use this because it will affect a deep childhood wound that you have had and it will make you question yourself and you will become motivated to do what will not make you appear selfish.

This tactic is quite popular among advertisers. A cosmetic company might make an individual feel old or unattractive. This tactic is also used in interpersonal relationships. For example, a person may make their romantic partner start thinking that they can never be loved by anybody else.

The silent treatment.
Although it is normal for an individual to verbally and emotionally shut down if they are getting overwhelmed emotionally, a manipulator can also use this as a tactic to manipulate someone. A manipulative individual will shut down connections and communication as a form of punishment. This may include withholding affection, intimacy, or any form of communication.

Changing the rules midway.
The manipulator might change a situation's rules midway through just to stop the victim from becoming successful. The rules could be something like highlighting elements that disqualify your success or giving additional stipulations that you need to be successful. A manipulative individual keeps the other individual in a constant state

of chasing the manipulator for their approval by using this tactic.

Withholding some truths.

A manipulator will manipulate the facts. They will blame you, make excuses, lie to you, or withhold some truths and strategically share some facts about them. When they do this, it makes them feel that they are in charge and have power over you. They also feel like they are becoming superior intellectually.

Making comparisons.

A manipulator can compare you to another individual to provoke you. They may make you feel insecure or make you feel like everyone else is doing that particular thing that you are not doing, but it is the manipulator who actually wants you to do that thing. They may compare you with a specific person, which can be annoying. They may even get other people to pressure you into doing a certain thing or getting a certain emotion out of you.

The triangulation tactic.

Triangulation is when a third individual is brought in to sway the side that wins when two people disagree. Triangulation is used by a manipulative individual to ensure that their side emerges the winner of an argument. They can achieve this by floating the information to make it more in favor of their side or choosing a third individual that they know will agree with them.

This makes the victim question the manipulative individual less frequently, and then they eventually put an end to asking the manipulator questions. The victim's feelings of isolation can also be increased with this, and this increases the victim's dependence on the manipulative individual.

Switching attention from themselves.

When there is an argument about a person's behavior, the person may switch the attention from themselves and change the subject by attacking their critic. This switching of attention may be the person saying something like, Well, what about your poor parenting skills? Or they may say, what about your drug abuse? In this case, the manipulative person takes the attention away from themselves to their partner's poor parenting skills or drug abuse.

The advantage of location.
A person who is manipulating you will attempt to get you out of your comfort zone and take you to a place you find unfamiliar and where they will be in control.

Love Bombing to build trust and intimacy.
A manipulator might control another individual's behavior through intense emotional connection.

For instance, an individual who is abusive may try to manipulate someone by making a romantic relationship move very quickly. They may display loving gestures to their victims to the point that they become overwhelmed with it or they may engage in love bombing to make their victim feel indebted and let down their guard.

Love bombing is when an individual bombards someone with intense emotions, affection, and excess energy and time. It may include spending a large part of one's energy and time pleasing the victim, making elaborate declarations of how one admires the victim, and giving the victim gifts. A manipulative individual quickly builds trust and intimacy with the victim through love bombing. The victim's natural desire to feel appreciated and wanted is preyed upon by the manipulator and it becomes a tool to increase devotion of the victim to them.

The gaslighting tactic.
Gaslighting is when a person makes you question yourself, including your feelings, sanity, trust in yourself, memory, and even your own identity. This may be manipulating situations to make you doubt

yourself or the abuser calling you crazy. A manipulative individual does this to make you automatically trust them and do what they ask you to do without asking them any questions, thereby giving them power and control over you.

Making generalizations.

When an individual's traits are applied to a whole group of people who are in the same demographic, it is known as generalization. For instance, a manipulator might say that all women pay more attention to themselves than their partners. When the manipulator says something like this, the victim is then encouraged to act in a way that the manipulator considers easiest to control or agreeable with them.

Controlling your daily activities and life.

Manipulation's goal is to have more control over you. But apart from controlling your behavior and how you feel, the manipulative individual is also able to shape what your daily activities and life look like. This can include restricting the friends you can spend time with, preventing you from continuing your education or even controlling access to your money. The goal of the manipulator in controlling your daily activities is to ensure that you feel like you cannot make decisions without them or function without them.

Giving diminishing or dismissive comments.

A manipulative individual can respond with a diminishing or dismissive comment when their victim makes a contribution that is valid during discussions in a group or when they achieve success. The manipulator does this to stay in control. It can be like giving reasons for why their victim's comment is unworthy of the consideration and attention of other people, or giving reasons for why the victim's success was not earned.

The projection tactic.

This involves a psychological defense mechanism where an individual puts their desires, characteristics, or feelings onto another individual. When the victim advocates doing something for themselves or presents alternative activities, the manipulator might say something like, you are so controlling. They take what they want and feel and project it onto the victim to avoid the feeling associated with it or how it makes them look.

Name-calling you.
A manipulative individual will often label the behavior of the victim or the victim's personality traits with negative verbiage. This is done to make the victim feel like they are not enough, and also to convince them that they do not deserve to be treated better. This usually begins in small ways that are not very offensive and then increases in frequency and intensity as the victim gets more used to the name-calling.

Guilt-tripping you.
A manipulative individual guilt-trips you to change how you feel. They might say something like, "If you choose to go out to the movies with your friend tonight, I will feel sad and lonely." The long-term goal of the manipulator is to get you to discuss that thing with them first in the future before doing it again.

Blaming their victim for the emotional abuse.
It is common for the manipulative individual to shut down a victim when they speak up about emotional abuse. They shut the victim down by telling them that they actually did something to earn the emotional manipulation they are experiencing. This then makes the victim always second guess their actions as they want to avoid having a negative interaction with the manipulative individual.

Changing the topic.
Changing topics is normal during conversations, but a manipulative individual uses this tactic to make an individual feel devalued or to punish an individual. When someone gives the victim a compliment or the victim makes a valid point during a conversation, a

manipulative individual will change the topic of the discussion to prevent the victim from gaining any confidence.

An emotional manipulator makes the victim question their own intelligence and abilities by ensuring that the victim feels like no one else can praise them other than the manipulator.

Treating you like you are less capable or a child.
A manipulative individual treats their victim like a child or like they are less capable. It is a form of gaslighting that reduces the trust that the victim has in themselves to take charge of responsibility.

It may be in the form of physically treating the victim like they are not capable of performing certain tasks, taking over a task from the victim when they are already in the middle of a task that they can do on their own, or talking down to the individual like they are not intelligent enough.

Using coercion or threats.
When an individual uses threats to convince you or force you to do something, you are being emotionally manipulated. This manipulation could include threats to take away something that you consider valuable and important or threats to leave you if you refuse to do what the individual wants you to do. The manipulator might even threaten to hurt themselves.

Although they may just be saying it and not actually want to hurt themselves, you need to always take threats that involve self-harm seriously. This is important. It is important that you maintain your boundaries for emotional and physical safety, and it is also important that you encourage the manipulator to get professional help if they threaten to harm themselves.

Constantly shifting the criteria.
This is when a manipulator constantly shifts the goalposts. They

keep shifting the criteria you must meet to satisfy them. For instance, a bully may harass their colleague at work by using their colleagues' clothes as an excuse to do that. If the colleague changes clothes because of the harassment, the bully may say that the colleague won't deserve to get professional respect until they also change their accent, hairstyle, or some other trait.

These forms of emotional manipulation may be combined by a manipulator or the manipulator may alternate between them depending on the situation.

Reasons for Manipulation

Not every manipulation is done with malicious intent, even when the manipulator's actions cause immense harm.

The following are some common reasons people engage in tactics of manipulation:
Absence of connection.
Some individuals use manipulation to control other people and treat these people as a means to an end. Sometimes, this is a sign that the individual has a personality disorder like a narcissistic personality.

Absence of effective communication skills.
Some individuals may not be comfortable with direct communication. Others may be from homes where manipulative communication was used.

Social needs.
There are some forms of manipulation that are beneficial and even normal. For instance, most people learn that being cheerful and friendly around co-workers is important to advance professionally.

A way to avoid blame.
People use manipulation to avoid blame. Although some individuals

avoid blame as a way to abuse another individual or control them, others avoid blame because they have low self-esteem, they fear judgment, or they struggle to face the shortcomings they have.

Manipulation as a result of fear.

Fear may make people manipulate others. The fear of abandonment is one of such fears. This usually occurs during relationship fights or breakups.

Advertising, marketing, and other political or financial incentives. Many industries are dedicated to manipulating the emotions of people to change their minds and get them to purchase products, or convince them to vote for a certain candidate or political party.

Many manipulators do not have effective communication skills. Or they might have been punished by an influential figure because they expressed their wants or needs. For this reason, the original means for connecting becomes replaced by strategies that are centered around staying away from any sense of fault. It is achieved through refusing to be accountable for actions and indirect communication.

Treatment for Manipulation

It can be difficult to identify manipulation or even admit when you are being manipulated. This is not your fault, and it can be hard for you to prevent it. But you can do some things that can help you reduce the emotional impact that manipulation can have on you.

You can set boundaries in a relationship by doing the following:

• Set boundaries to tackle manipulation and look for how to let the manipulator know that you are aware that they are manipulating you, and that you no longer want to take part in the conversation.
• Communication should be specific, direct, and clear.
• Look for someone you trust, who is not being influenced by the

manipulator, and ask them to give you advice concerning the situation.

- Know when manipulation should be addressed.

When you are able to identify manipulation, you have solved a large part of the problem. If it is a loved one that is manipulating you, it can be hard to seek help. But manipulation is capable of affecting your emotional well-being. So, finding a safe way to solve the problem is important.

If you have feelings of being manipulated by someone, whether the person is a friend, relative, co-worker, partner, or anyone else, getting help is important. And you need to get help, especially if you notice that the situation is abusive in any way. You can talk to a friend, therapist, relationship counselor, or trusted family member.

CHAPTER TWO:
Embracing Your Identities

Every one of us has multiple identities, and those identities continue competing for primacy in our heads. We could help make the world a better place by learning to celebrate our complex identities.

There are different groups that compete for our attention and even demand to have the top spot in our lives. That includes political parties that influence our choices, musical styles that influence lifestyles, and companies that attempt to make their brands part of us, not to mention the different claims to gender, racial, and group loyalty.

When a group considers you disloyal, it can have severe consequences, since human beings allocate resources such as welfare support and housing, and emotional resources like compassion and empathy, through their groups. During times of war, deciding which identity to be loyal to can be difficult because it can be a matter of life and death.

And yet, evidence shows that our world would be a more peaceful and better place if we had space for different identities in ourselves as well as other individuals. How can you do this and try not to elevate one over all the others during times of conflict?

Take a look at the following tips:

Multiple identities are normal.
For many generations, rich politicians have positioned themselves as "one of you," while putting up policies that only benefited a small number of people, who are also rich people. Individuals march in public for gender or racial equality while privately acting in ways that increase gender and racial inequality.

Most people won't see this as news but let it be a reminder that things are always not as simple as they might appear to be. When you call yourself a progressive, it does not mean that every action you take or every word you say leads to progress, and becoming a Christian does not mean that you have become free of sin. Some individuals claim that when you join a group it will bring you many privileges. But after joining the group, you notice that things are not the way they presented them to be. You discover that they have manipulated you into joining the group and doing things that are in their own interest and not in your best interest.

We are complex individuals. We have identities that are sometimes conflicting as well as impulses that can lead to behavior that contradicts the words we say. This is a normal thing. Although there might not be a group that you can join that will take away all the problems you have in your life and the problems in the entire world, a complex social life that welcomes multiple identities can give you enormous richness.

You can belong to different groups, and other people can also do the same. Life is made interesting when the multiple identities we have come together to shape our behavior and decisions.

Separate likability from credibility

Every one of us has been there. You are walking down your street and see somebody walking past you with the exact shirt you are wearing and you feel an instant connection with the individual. You belong to the same group.

Having those feelings is not bad. Nothing is wrong with it. People are usually happy when they randomly find others like this, and this part of human life is charming. But during serious discussions, every one of us needs to be wary of commonalities that are not relevant to the present topic.

Whether you want to acknowledge it or you don't want to

acknowledge it, you often prefer individuals who are similar in interests, personality, intellect, demographics, and education to you. But just because a person listens to the same music that you listen to does not mean that the opinion they have about gas prices is more valid than the opinion of another person who listens to music that you don't like.

For this reason, likability needs to be separated from credibility, and we need to watch out for bias that may be present within ourselves against random in-groups and for random in-groups.

Find the truth.
Everybody feels intense social pressure to act and think in ways that are consistent with group activities that are important.

One major warning sign is when you join a group and you feel compelled to mislead other people or lie, especially about other groups. When that compulsion to lie to go along with the herd is present, you need to tell yourself that the group is not you and you are not the group. And you need to remind yourself that you need to find the truth and what is accurate in the group.

You need to ask questions if the group is focused on outsiders.

Groups may face communal threats even though not all the threats they get are serious ones. Some threats might be imaginary.

Leaders who are hungry for power know that fear is a powerful tool used by manipulators. A leader may mobilize fear against another group of people or turn their people into a threat against another group, thereby helping them to rise to power.

Fear can be misused. So, how can you know that it is being misused?

First, you need to name the emotion and also acknowledge that you feel afraid because of what you heard. Watch the fear you have without judgment. You can ask yourself if your fear is of specific acts or if your fear is of a whole group of people. Are you threatened personally? Is there any evidence of the threat? Is there any evidence that shows they are not a threat? Do you have any identities in common? Can you look for other things in common with them that would lead to a reduction in the threat? How can you respond courageously to this potential threat? Do you share any goals? How can you replace your fear with courage?

You might discover that fear is baseless or you might discover that it is saying that there is a real threat. You can avoid being manipulated by paying attention to what is going on around you.

Appreciate the multiple identities in others and in yourself.

When you identify with a group, there will be pressure to behave in some particular ways, and you will notice that you are usually supporting norms that the group has accepted and norms that are common in the group. But many of us usually identify with more than one group, and it's okay. We identify with different groups, values, and norms that sometimes come into conflict with each other. And even as they conflict with each other, they still combine to give us our identity.

If visitors from outside the town or a unique event is what activates a strong group identity, you will discover that there is a change in someone's personality. On Friday, a friend might be talking fast, swearing, and also teasing to show affection, but then come to church on Sunday and then become suddenly different and quiet.

Identity shifts are important to us. If you are spending time with your children at the playground, the social role of parenting in the midst of other parents is what your sense of self is linked to. If you travel to another country and then attend an international food festival, seeing the different foods on display from your country will make you feel strong ties to your roots. You might be a cyclist back in your country. So, when you go for a bike ride, it will make you identify as a member of the cyclist community. You will identify with surfers if you surf. You will also have times when you need to connect with other parents and then advocate for the common interests you have. A day might come when you connect with other surfers or cyclists for a personal cause as well.

These different identities which span across talents, values, strengths, interests, and social roles make up who we are.

That insight can be used by you as a way to connect effectively with other people, even if those people first appear to be outsiders. It is important that we appreciate the numerous social categories that exist. If you are not a cyclist or you don't surf, you might connect with another individual over parenthood. If you cannot connect over parenthood because you are not a parent, surfing might be a common thing for you and the other individual.

Beyond individual connection moments, research shows that when a group embraces individuals who are different and encourages their group members to embrace unique identities that exist beyond the self, they can make better decisions. Wherever you are in the world, no individual possesses an identity that is only limited to nationality. Multiple identities are multiple opportunities, and you need to see things this way instead of seeing the multiple identities as threats to unity.

CHAPTER THREE:
The World of Dark Psychology

This should not freak you out. It is possible to know beyond words what people intend to say. You can sense what they mean from their heart even when they say something else. Your personal, social, and work life will be significantly affected by your ability to read people correctly. When you have an understanding of how another individual is feeling, your communication style and message can then be adapted to make sure that the other individual receives the message in the best way possible. This is not that difficult. Although this may appear cliché, no special powers are needed if you want to read people.

Dark psychology is how people use psychological tactics to manipulate other people and control them. It is the study of human nature's dark side or the psychological mechanisms that make people engage in manipulative, harmful, or antisocial behaviors. This topic is both a disturbing and fascinating one that explores the reasons why some individuals abuse, cheat, lie, steal, or even kill others.

Dark psychology techniques have been used to manipulate and control people by individuals in positions of power. It has been in existence for centuries. Today, people often associate it with psychopaths, sociopaths, and narcissists as they often use these techniques to achieve their desires.

Have you been longing to read people with tricks from psychology? The following tips will help you read individuals like a pro:

Notice people's appearance.
Do your best to notice peoples' appearance when you are reading

them. Pay attention to the clothes they are wearing. Are they putting on a T-shirt and jeans, which signifies comfort? Or they are dressed for success, which shows that they are ambitious?

Are they wearing a pendant such as a Buddha or cross which means they have spiritual values? You can sense something from whatever they are wearing. Ensure that you notice any identity claims. Identity claims are deliberate statements people make about their goals, attitudes, values, etc. and they include things such as rings, tattoos, or a t-shirt with slogans. An important thing to remember about identity statements is that because the identity statements are deliberate, a lot of individuals assume you are being disingenuous and manipulative with them, but there is very little evidence concerning this. The thing is, people usually want to be known. And they will even do their best to be known even at the expense of looking good. If they have to make a choice between being seen authentically and being seen positively, they would choose to be seen authentically instead.

Also, some studies show that people can read psychological traits at least to a certain degree on an individual's face.

A person with higher extraversion levels had more protruding lips and nose, masseter muscles, and a chin that is recessive. On the other hand, a person with lower levels of extraversion has a face in which the area that is found around the nose seems to press against the person's face. These studies show that perhaps psychological traits can to a certain degree be read on the face of an individual, though more research is required to gain an understanding of this phenomenon.

Stay open-minded and objective.
Before you start trying to read people, the first thing to do is to work on having an open mind. Your past experiences and emotions should not be allowed to influence your opinions and impressions.

If you are quick to judge people, you will misread them. So, you need to be objective when approaching every situation and interaction. You won't get the whole story about someone when you use logic alone. You need some other important forms of information as you will be able to learn to use them to read the non-verbal cues that individuals give off. If you want to see somebody clearly, you need to stay objective and be able to receive information neutrally and not distort it.

Don't avoid small talk.

Maybe you don't feel comfortable with small talk. However, this can give you the opportunity to become familiar with the other individual.

Small talk makes it easy for you to watch closely how an individual behaves during normal situations. This can then be a benchmark that will help you accurately discover any of a person's behavior that is out of the ordinary. One error that individuals make when trying to read people is that they don't get a baseline of their normal behavior.

Be attentive and notice people's posture.

You can learn a lot about an individual's attitude from their posture. The person is confident if they walk with their head held high. However, they may have low self-esteem if they walk in an indecisive manner.

When you are looking at a person's posture, see if the person walks in an indecisive manner as it means that they have issues with their self-esteem, or if they walk with their head held high as it indicates that they are confident.

Pay attention to the words and tone a person uses.

When you are talking to an individual, pay attention to the words they use. When the person says "This is my third promotion," they are telling you that they have been promoted twice before. One thing you should know is that people like this often rely on other people to boost their self-image. They are hoping that you will praise them so that it can boost their self-image and make them feel good about themselves.

It is important that you also pay attention to the tone used. The tone a person uses and the volume of their voice can reveal a lot about their emotions. Vibrations are created by sound frequencies. When reading individuals, pay attention to how their voice tone affects you. Ask yourself if the person's tone feels soothing or if it is whiny, snippy, or abrasive.

Pay attention to the physical movements they make.

People express their feelings more through their movements than their words. For instance, we often lean towards the people we like and move away from the people we do not like. One good sign is if a person is leaning in, their palms facing up, and hands out and open. This indicates that the person is connecting with you. If you notice that the individual is leaning away, it indicates that they are putting up a wall.

Another physical movement you can look out for is the crossing of legs or arms. If you notice that someone is crossing their legs or arms, it indicates anger, defensiveness, or self-protection. If a person is leaning in and you say something and they cross their arms all of a sudden, it means that you said something that the individual does not like.

On the other hand, if a person is hiding their hands, it indicates that the person is hiding something. But if you notice that the person is cuticle picking or lip biting, it indicates that they are in an awkward situation or trying to soothe themselves under pressure.

Ask questions that are direct to receive a straight answer.

If you want to receive a straight answer, you have to avoid asking questions that are vague. Ensure that you don't interrupt when the individual is providing an answer to your question. Instead, observe their mannerisms as they speak. You can gain valuable insight into how an individual thinks from action words.

For instance, if someone says that they have decided to choose a particular brand, "decided" is the action word. The word shows that the person has weighed different options, the person is not impulsive, and they usually think things through. Action words help you understand how an individual thinks.

Pay attention to your gut.

When you first meet someone, it is important to listen to your gut. Before you even get a chance to think, this will give you a visceral reaction. Your gut can help you know whether you are at ease or not with the individual.

They occur quickly, helping you know if you can trust people. They are your internal truth meter.

Stay alert and notice flashes of insight.

Sometimes, there may be an ah-ha moment about someone. You need to pay attention because the insights come in a flash. We often miss it because we move rapidly on to the next thought and we lose these critical insights.

Avoid assumptions.

When you make assumptions and are not sure of something, it can lead to misunderstanding. There may be more trouble if you simply make assumptions without having a full understanding of the other person. People can make errors when they make assumptions when reading others. One such error is not being conscious of biases.

For instance, if you simply assume that someone is angry, then whatever that person does or says will appear to be concealed anger to you. You don't have to jump to conclusions when your spouse doesn't watch your favorite TV show with you but goes to bed. Don't think that they don't want to spend time with you; they may just be tired and want to rest. If you want to read people like a pro, you need to keep your mind positive and open, and you also need to relax.

Sense the individual's presence.
What this means is that you need to feel the emotional atmosphere surrounding you. Try to notice if someone you are reading has a presence that is making you back off if they have a friendly presence that pulls you closer to them, or if you face a wall. The energy we emit is referred to as presence, and it is not necessarily congruent with behavior or words.

You can feel goosebumps.
You can have goosebumps when you resonate with individuals who inspire or move you. You can also have goosebumps if what an individual is saying strikes a chord within you. Music, movies, and moving experiences seem to trigger it.

Also, you can feel goosebumps when you experience deja vu, which is a recognition that you have known a person before, even though you have never met the person.

Scan the overall behavior of the person.
People sometimes make the assumption that if a certain action is done, like when a person is looking down at the floor when having a conversation, it shows that they are anxious or nervous.

But familiarity with a person will help you know whether they are just relaxing when they look down on the floor or when they avoid eye contact. People have different ways in which they behave, and some of these behaviors that people have are simply mannerisms. This is what makes creating a baseline of the normal behavior of others helpful. Learn how you can identify any deviation from the usual behavior that a person has. When you discover that there is a change in their body language, pace, or tone, you will know that something is not right.

Observe people's eyes.

Have you ever heard people say that the eyes are the doorway to people's souls? Our eyes transmit energies that are powerful. So, ensure that you carefully watch people's eyes. What do you see when you observe someone's eyes? Do you see a guarded, angry, or mean person? Or do you see a caring person? A person's eyes can reveal whether they are telling the truth or lying. When you look at someone's pupil size, you can also tell if they like something.

Practice studying people.

You will become perfect with practice. When you practice studying people, you will be able to read them more accurately with time. Do this exercise where you practice putting talk shows on mute while watching them. Observing their actions and facial expressions will help you see what individuals are feeling when they are speaking, without hearing anything they are saying. Then, put the volume on and watch again to see if your observation was right.

Try to interpret the person's facial expressions.

Unless you have mastered the poker face, you will usually have your emotions showing on your face. You can interpret facial expressions in a variety of ways. They include:

When you notice that deep frown lines are forming, it means that the individual is overthinking or worried. On the other hand, you will notice crow's feet, which are the smile lines of joy in an individual who is truly laughing.

One other thing to watch out for is if the person's lips are pursed, which can signal contempt, anger, or bitterness. Also, when a person is grinding their teeth or has a clenched jaw, it means they are tense.

The following is a classification of smiles in psychology today:

The reward smile: This is when the individual's lips are pulled directly upwards, eyebrows lift, and dimples at the sides of the mouth. This shows positive feedback.

The affiliative smile: This is when the individual presses their lips together and at the same time has little dimples at the side of their mouth. It signifies liking and friendship.

The dominance smile: This is when the individual's upper lip is raised with their cheeks being pushed upwards, there is a deepening of the indentation between the nose and the mouth, the upper lids are raised, and there is a wrinkling of the nose.

It is important that you know how to read people. Reading people makes you sensitive to people's needs and struggles. Learning this skill will help you boost your EQ. Anyone can read people. You only need to be aware of what to look for.

Analyzing Individuals with Dark Psychology

Are you triggered? Is somebody constantly showing raging anger? Are you being triggered and continuously taken advantage of? Do you frequently get anxious and feel somebody is emotionally insensitive? You may be searching for something to see if the individual is trustworthy or not.

Studies show that whenever you see an individual that has a dark personality, there is an amygdala activation and your mind and body become instantly aware.

The amygdala, which becomes active whenever a person's body

perceives a threat, is a flight and fight response center of the brain. The brain learns these traits over our human race's evolution. So, you will often get triggered when dealing with individuals with dark personalities.

When you use dark psychology, you will see that it is capable of helping you know why people make certain decisions or behave the way they do. You can use dark psychology to predict a person's future behavior by studying their past behavior. You can use this in a variety of situations such as predicting the performance of employees or predicting the behavior of customers. You can also use dark psychology to identify patterns in an individual's behavior that you may not notice at first glance. You will understand why people take certain actions and make certain decisions when you study the patterns over time. Also, dark psychology makes it possible for you to see how a person's overall behavior or decision-making process can be affected by different factors.

You will find dark psychology important when it comes to understanding human behavior and analyzing their behavior from a scientific perspective. It makes it possible for researchers to gain a deeper understanding of why individuals behave the way they do by paying attention to and studying over time the processes that are both conscious and unconscious. When researchers utilize techniques of dark psychology, they are able to better predict future behaviors from past behaviors and also identify patterns in the behavior of individuals that may not be noticed immediately. A greater potential for unlocking the mysteries that surround human thought processes comes with the ever-increasing popularity of dark psychology, and this could benefit every one of us for many years to come.

Dark Psychology combines psychopathy, narcissism, and Machiavellianism. Therefore, you need to essentially analyze these factors when you want to analyze people with dark psychology.

Some individuals are evil-minded. They see life as a chessboard, and they use the individuals around them as pawns. They will do anything to win a trophy.

These cold-blooded toxic and cunning people will strip your identity away, give you an image, and also give you a cheerleader role that you will play for them. They are your masters and saviors.

The dark psychology triad is about three personality traits that are connected to manipulative and malicious behaviors.

The personality traits include:

The Machiavellianism trait.

Machiavellianism consists of a set of personality traits associated with deceptive and manipulative behaviors. It is named after Niccolo Machiavelli, who was an Italian Renaissance politician known for his deceitful and cunning political strategies. People high in Machiavellianism are skilled at navigating social situations to their advantage. These people are often strategic and manipulative.

You would come in contact with a person or the other in social life or the workplace with such personalities who manipulate, trigger, or irritate you. This person may be your romantic partner, colleague, or boss. You may be trying to learn how to identify people with dark psychology because you suspect that there is a person in your life with a dark personality. Machevallianism, which is a manipulation trait, is something a dark triad would have. You will also feel that you are constantly being manipulated by the individual whom you believe has a dark personality.

Is manipulation and deception the same? Deception and manipulation may get you confused. Are you being manipulated?

Firstly, we need to understand what causes the so-called dark personality.

The narcissism trait.

This personality trait is characterized by a need for validation and admiration, a lack of empathy for other individuals, and an inflated sense of self-importance. Narcissists believe that they should be given special treatment because they are special. Their sense of entitlement causes them to mistreat other people and exploit them to achieve their own goals. They may also be resentful, arrogant, and envious.

If you are concerned about getting an analysis of a dark personality, you may have presumed that the individual you are trying to analyze may be a narcissist. Two particular reasons exist for it; one is that the internet is filled with ideas, videos, and articles about narcissism, and the second is the attractiveness, charmingness, charm, and aura of the narcissist. Narcissists are manipulators.

The difference between narcissism and a dark triad and psychology is a dark personality looks for an object's benefit like work, sex, or money, while a narcissist often looks for a victim and seeks your emotional energy.

A dark personality squeezes the resources you have, while a narcissist drains your emotions. You are dealing with a dark triad when an individual has some traits that are matching with a narcissist, but many traits are not.

Codependency syndrome is an important character trait that attracts narcissists. Codependency involves your personality vulnerability through which you become dependent on a narcissist. So, your own vulnerabilities are one thing you should look out for.

An online codependency test can help you find out if you are codependent or not. If you have a moderate codependency scale, you have a lower probability of being with a narcissist, and so if you are with a person, who may be triggering you, then the individual has a higher likelihood of having multiple dark personality traits.

The psychopathy trait.

This personality disorder is marked by a deficiency in empathy, remorse, and conscience. Psychopaths often have high impulsivity and a superficial charm. These people may exhibit aggressive, antisocial, and violent behaviors without thinking about the consequences of their actions. They may also be parasitic, irresponsible, and callous.

Understanding gender differences is one essence of dark psychology analysis. The individual who has triggered you to search for dark psychology is probably someone who is bossy.

You might feel like the bossy person is excessively dominating you. Females that have a high level of psychopathy, and who are also in a position of leadership have a strong negative correlation with transformational leadership. So, the person is not able to transform an organization or system effectively even when they are bossy.

Therefore, If a female is bossy and is in a leadership position, but no visible transformation or visible impact exists, then she may be high on the dark triad.

Impulsivity and dominance.

Impulsivity and fearless dominance are two important traits of psychopathy.

If you have witnessed impulsive reactions that were sudden and the individual appears to be more fearless than the people around you, it means that the probability of a very high trait of psychopathy is high. In addition, an individual who has a high psychopathy trait has an affinity for pain. They like to either receive pain or give pain. This involves emotional pain, which is associated with narcissists, as well as physical pain.

So, if you have witnessed the individual causing physical boundary breaching, throwing things, and taking or giving physical pain, you may be dealing with an individual with a dark triad and personality.

Using Biology to Analyze Dark Psychology

Knowing the biology of a dark personality trait is also important because biology is responsible for many of their behaviors. Since a distinct different genetic and brain pattern is present in any mental disorder, a distinct biological pattern is bound to be present. One key trait of a dark personality is the desire to achieve more. This makes them have low pre-frontal cortex activation as well as low consciousness. A behavior's consequence is analyzed by the prefrontal cortex.

Our consciousness hormone is serotonin. Therefore, PFC is activated by this hormone. Hence an individual with a dark psychology, dark personality, and the dark triad will have low consciousness as well as serotonin. This is referred to as the serotonin syndrome.

You need to know the following:
1. Dopamine and serotonin hormones are responsible for neuroplasticity and link the cerebellum, prefrontal cortex, and hippocampus. Therefore, the DTP possesses very low dopamine and serotonin. And they are always moody and unhappy.
2. Their thermal regulation is gone as a result of the lack of serotonin. Therefore, they are cold-blooded and warmth is absent when you are touched by them.
3. The HPA axis is activated by the midbrain and has high adrenaline. Therefore, they are angry, aggressive, and raging with expressed or suppressed violence.
4. Research has shown that people who are pathological liars lack prefrontal cortex activation. The mid-brain mostly manages it.
5. Acidosis is caused by hypothermic blood. This leads to tissue necrosis. So, several skin problems continue to exist. They have the

feeling of cold, which makes them hydrophobic, thereby resulting in avoiding washing and baths.

6. Because the somatic nervous system is also regulated by serotonin, there is poor muscle control. An inability to do small works like threading a needle, tremors, or a weak handshake.

7. Ectopic heartbeat and palpitations are caused by hypothermia. So, they get very anxious and are always afraid.

8. Because high neuron activation, which gets impaired as a result of serotonin deficiency and leads to minerals being absorbed in low amounts, is needed by gut wall peristalsis, physical strength, muscles, and bones are reduced.

9. Serotonin makes it hard for them to sleep early.

10. They are skeptical of reality as a result of a lack of PFC activation. This makes them stalkers and detectives.

11. Vasoconstriction is caused by high adrenaline, resulting in very high blood pressure.

12. They do their best to use confidence to overcome this fear. This mask comes off when they are under stress and their response becomes violent.

13. The kidney is unable to remove such a large amount of waste. Therefore, stinking body odor is developed, thereby becoming toxic.

14. They don't have any solid memory, so they create stories to make sense of their life. It is only those things that satisfy their stories that they remember.

15. A hypertensive father, who is highly aggressive, and a depressed mother who made some compromises to maintain the family, leading to DTP.

Using biology to analyze dark psychology:

• Their body temperature may be low, and when they are given a body touch such as a handshake, the handshake may feel very cold.

• They may be highly conscious of their image, thereby their brand of consciousness may be very high.

• They may suffer from some allergies such as itching.

• They may suffer from hydrophobia, thereby making them avoid baths.

- Their natural body odor may be very bad and they may resort to using fragrance.
- They may have hypertension.
- They may not be sleeping early at night, and dark circles would be seen in their eyes as a result of staying awake till late at night.

Using Behavioural and Social Traits to Analyze Dark Personality

The signature of all the criminals is pretty much the Dark Triad. Personality(DTP). These individuals convince themselves that they are without guilt and they are good people, while they are full of lies and manipulation. What they say and do differ greatly.

As long as you agree to what they want, they are very nice. However, when you start to disagree with what they want, they get angry and shun you down with their anger and words.

They make you afraid. They have extreme envy, jealousy, and hatred. They do their best to act as the victims in every situation. They blame you for everything, and they shame-trip and guilt-trip you. They don't really feel sorry when they say they are sorry. This is because serotonin, which connects the entire brain, is needed for feeling.

They find it hard to do something for long as they get easily bored. They start doing something but never complete it. They are afraid of reality. They stalk you to get all the information.

They will always appear smart and silently instigate you against those close to you and your loved ones. They will try to look for shortcuts to achieve success. You will experience a kind of chill feeling and your gut will tell you. Yet, you will not pay attention and listen to anybody.

So, an individual who finds it boring to do the same work over and over again, and who is always seeking out new things that they can do to take away their boredom, may have a dark Psychology.

Once you have DTP, there is no going away as it is an addiction. Your mind stays hostage forever.

Are you hoping that they will change? This disorder is clinically irreversible. Your serotonin shouldn't be depleted by you hating, hoping, and getting hurt. You need to run as far as you can.

Understanding Manipulation and Dark Psychology in Relationships

The field of psychology covers a variety of topics, all looking to elucidate the human mind and human behavior's complexities. While a large part of this work is focused on positive elements such as personal development as well as mental health and well-being, a darker side also exists in psychology. The realm of dark psychology is this shadowy corner. But what exactly is it, and what is the manifestation like in our daily lives?

Dark psychology involves the scientific study of human behavior's darker aspects. The human behavior includes deceit, control, manipulation, coercion, and persuasion. It usually investigates actions that are ethically and morally wrong, especially those actions that are aimed at harming other people or exploiting them. It is sometimes connected to studies about "dark triad" personality traits, and they include psychopathy, Machiavellianism, and narcissism.

The idea behind dark psychology is to have a full understanding of these behaviors that are harmful and not to glorify them. When you study them, you will be able to come up with ways to identify and protect yourself and others against them.

Manipulation is an important part of dark psychology. Manipulative behaviors that people display may range from emotional manipulation that is subtle to tactics that are blatant and overt. Guilt-tripping, playing the victim, psychological bullying, gaslighting, or using fear as a control tactic, are some of these actions.

A case of manipulation and dark psychology might involve an individual in a position of power, such as the CEO of a company, using the position they have as the CEO to influence or control their subordinates in an unfair manner. This could be in the form of playing favorites, subtly threatening job security, or exploiting the employees' personal information for their own advantage.

Manipulators usually understand human emotions deeply and use this knowledge that they have to play with the feelings of others and control the way they respond. This can lead to severe psychological and emotional damage to the individual who is on the receiving end of those tactics.

Dark psychology is a field of psychology that is based on understanding, analyzing, as well as manipulating the behavior of people. It has been in existence for centuries, but its popularity is increasing as the world becomes more interconnected and complex.

The study of the behavior of humans from a scientific perspective is referred to as dark psychology. It involves gaining insight into how individuals think and act by using research methods such as surveys, psychological tests, interviews, and observational studies. It considers both conscious as well as unconscious processes in order to have a better understanding of why people take the actions they take.

Dark psychology is based on two main principles at its core. They include persuasion and manipulation. Persuasion involves trying to convince a person to change their opinion of something through emotional appeals or logical arguments, while manipulation involves gaining control over another individual through the use of your influence or power. Manipulation usually relies on coercion or deception. Both manipulation and persuasion are used in dark psychology.

Using psychological tactics to influence decision-making or behavior is another major concept in dark psychology. These psychological tactics can vary from subtle suggestions or hints to more overt types of manipulation like fearmongering. The idea is always to get another person to do the particular thing you want them to do, not minding if it is not in their own best interests.

Dark psychology is used in many areas, and it is used in both professional and personal settings. It can be used personally for self-advancement purposes or it can be used to manipulate other people for one's advantage. It can be used professionally for deal negotiations, sales techniques, and marketing purposes. Law enforcement officers also use dark psychology during interrogations and politicians use it during their speeches and debates in order to persuade the audience in the direction they want them to go.

There are numerous ways in which dark psychology can manifest in relationships. These ways include gaslighting, manipulation, emotional abuse, or even physical violence. These tactics are usually used by abusers to control their partners and exert power over their partners, thereby creating an environment that is toxic.

One partner in a relationship may control the other partner through emotional manipulation. For instance, they may constantly belittle the feelings of their partner, telling them that they are too sensitive or overreacting, or even making them feel guilty because they expressed their needs. A power imbalance is created in the relationship, and this can cause emotional damage.

In a case such as this, the victim often feels confused, powerless, or trapped, doubting their memories or experiences as a result of the tactics of the manipulator. Understanding dark psychology's signs can make it possible for people to spot such harmful behaviors if they exist in their relationships and then get help.

Manipulation Techniques of Dark Psychology

Intimidation and fear.
This can be likened to the bully who threatens to take a person's lunch money. They use fear to achieve their desire instead of using their words to get it. This is not a good way to play.

Guilt-tripping as a technique of dark psychology.
Has a close friend ever made you feel guilty whenever you were unable to hang out? Your friend might say something like, "I think I will just spend time alone at home then." This is a guilt trip.

The love-bombing and devaluation technique.
This is when you get a ton of compliments from a person, and then they start making criticisms about whatever you do. It's often hurtful and confusing, and often like a roller coaster of emotions.

Distraction and misdirection.
Imagine this like a magician who keeps you distracted with what they are doing with one hand and it takes your focus away from what the other hand is doing. Individuals using this technique might decide to do something dramatic or change the subject to distract you and take your focus away from the present thing that is happening.

Gaslighting as a technique of dark psychology.
Imagine if a person began to question your memories and they tell you that events that you know happened and clearly remember never took place. This is what gaslighting is. It works just like a magic

trick made to cause you to doubt your memories.

Gaslighting is a common manipulative tactic linked to dark psychology. It is a kind of psychological abuse whereby an individual makes another individual question their memories, perception of reality, or sanity.

Gaslighting involves making an individual always second-guess themselves, even questioning their reality or judgment. The people who use dark psychological tactics have this as a powerful tool in their arsenal, thereby leading to confusion and immense emotional distress.

Gaslighting might happen in a romantic relationship where one of the partners in the relationship always questions the other partner's memory. For example, the partner may deny that some events took place or they may even deny that they made certain promises, insisting that their partner is the one overreacting or misremembering. With time, this can make the victim start doubting their own sanity or memory.

Control of information.
Have you ever been in a position where everybody else appeared to know what was going on but your friend kept you in the dark about those things? That is control of information. This is just like the case where you are the last person to hear the gossip that has been around, but on a scale that is more serious.

Exploitation of affection and trust.
Do you have a friend who knows you would do anything to make them happy, and they use that to exploit your affection and trust to their advantage? It's like having a secret weapon they can use to get their way.

Endless criticisms.
Picture an individual who continues to make snide comments about

44

you, but later turns around and pretends like they are the only one who really understands you. It's just like having an individual who is your friend but continues to point out that there is spinach in your teeth but doesn't offer you a mirror to see it.

Dark Psychology and the Evil Label

It is important that we remember that psychology when looked at as a discipline seeks to gain an objective understanding of human behavior without applying labels such as "evil" or "good."

Dark psychology studies tendencies and behaviors that are undoubtedly unethical and harmful, but when we label dark psychology as "evil," the complex issues at hand could be oversimplified. Instead, it is best viewed as a tool to understand human behavior's harmful aspects to mitigate or prevent their effects.

The "evil" label is usually subjective and it can depend on personal or cultural values. However, the actions often associated with dark psychology have a harmful impact. For example, a company head who knowingly spreads false rumors to boost their own status and undermine competitors is displaying harmful and unethical actions even though their actions may not be necessarily "evil."

Facts of Dark Psychology

• Dark psychology is connected to the "dark triad" of personality traits, which include psychopathy, Machiavellianism, and narcissism. Individuals who possess these traits usually show tendencies for deceit, manipulation, and a lack of empathy. Dark psychology's relevance in understanding human behavior that is harmful is demonstrated by the facts around dark psychology. For instance, an individual displaying the dark triad's traits may regularly demonstrate behavior that is manipulative. This individual may deceive other people for their own personal gain, show a sense of entitlement, and show little remorse for their behavior.

• Dark psychology encompasses unethical and harmful behaviors, even though it is not evil per se.

• Dark psychology represents harmful behaviors collections that are widely studied, and this field is not formally recognized within psychology.

• Tactics of dark psychology like gaslighting are capable of causing individuals to question their own perception of reality.

Dark psychology reminds us of human behavior's complexities. It highlights the importance of recognizing and understanding destructive and manipulative behaviors to protect society and individuals from their effects. Although the field is dark, it is capable of shedding light on the things we need to do to implement a safer, healthier society.

Dark Psychology Benefits

1. Dark psychology makes it possible for you to understand why individuals do the things they do.

2. Improvement in the ability to detect manipulation, deception, or coercion by other individuals, and defend against them. It also includes the ability to shield oneself from exploitation or harm.

3. Enhanced competencies and skills in different domains that require psychological knowledge as well as insight, such as education, security, or law enforcement.

4. Increase in understanding of behavior and nature, especially the often ignored or hidden darker aspects. The benefits also include an increase in awareness.

Dark Psychology Harmful Effects

Dark psychology can also be harmful to people and society even though it can be intriguing and fascinating.

5. It can lead to an increase in violence and aggression: Individuals who practice dark psychology may lack remorse, empathy, or

conscience for their actions. They may see other people as objects or tools that they can use for their own gain, and pay no attention to these people's feelings or rights. They may have narcissism, superiority, or a sense of entitlement as well that makes them harm others and feel justified for doing that. This can result in homicide, criminal activity, or antisocial behavior in the dark psychology perpetrators.

6. It can affect rationality and decision-making: Individuals who are exposed to tactics of dark psychology such as persuasion, misinformation, or propaganda can be influenced to take actions that are against their own values or best interests. These individuals can be swayed by fear-mongering, false promises, or emotional appeals, and lose their independent and critical thinking ability. This can lead to guilt, regret, or poor choices in the dark psychology victims.

7. It can damage relationships and trust: Individuals who use techniques of dark psychology such as gaslighting, lying, or emotional manipulation can destroy the trust and bond they have developed with other individuals. They can cause others to doubt their judgments, feelings, and reality, and create a sense of insecurity and confusion. This can lead to anxiety, low self-esteem, emotional distress, and depression in the dark psychology victims.

Protecting Yourself from the Negative Effects of Dark Psychology

Stay informed and aware: The first thing to do to shield yourself from the negative effects that dark psychology can cause is to be aware that it exists and know its signs. Study the different strategies and techniques, such as persuasion, deception, hypnosis, gaslighting, and lying, that the practitioners of dark psychology use to manipulate other people. Learn how to identify and resist these tactics. Look for reliable information sources and verify any facts or claims before accepting them.

Be confident and assertive: After becoming informed and

aware, the next step to take if you want to protect yourself from the negative effects of dark psychology is to be proactive as well as confident in your own values and identity. Do not allow other people to tell you what to think or do. They should not define you. Stand up for your rights and what you believe in. Express your feelings and opinions respectfully and clearly. Feel free to disagree with others or say no when necessary. Trust your intuition and instincts, and do not give other people the opportunity to make you doubt your reality or yourself.

Be supportive and selective: The next step after being confident and assertive is to be supportive and selective in your social circles and relationships. Choose respectful, trustworthy, and honest individuals, and those who care for you and others. Avoid abusive, manipulative, or dishonest individuals, or those who are toxic towards you or others. Get support from your family members, friends, or professionals if you feel that dark psychology is affecting you or if you need help handling the effects of dark psychology.

The field of dark psychology is controversial and complex and it brings up many moral and ethical questions. Approaching it with caution as well as critical thinking is important. Balancing it with positive psychology is also important. Positive psychology has to do with studying human nature's positive aspects. It focuses on topics such as resilience, gratitude, happiness, purpose, compassion, well-being, optimism, altruism, resilience, and meaning. Its aim is to promote social good and human flourishing.

CHAPTER FOUR:
Making the Best of Body Language

Body language is something powerful that can be used in the workplace. You just need to use it to your advantage. We will discuss how this nonverbal communication tool can be used in the workplace.

There are different things to look at when conducting yourself, whether it is in your workplace or for an interview. Verbal as well as nonverbal communication plays a major role in this. Perhaps body language is a nonverbal form of communication that is very important. It is easy to notice when a person displays body language that is friendly or hostile, but how can these cues be used to your advantage?

It is important that you first understand what makes body language important. A large percentage of communication that humans make is nonverbal. What this means is that, when you smile with others, you will easily develop an instant connection with them than when you simply say "hello." Using hand gestures can place more emphasis on something than simply using words. And when you stand and your feet are in a wide stance, it shows that you are confident, and this subconsciously makes you be trusted by listeners. Body language has the capability to convey our intentions and emotions in ways that words are not able to. It is a powerful tool.

Body language usually sends a strong message, and it might even send a message that is stronger than the words you are saying aloud. This means that we can use our bodies to control how people perceive us. It is not only our voices we can use for communication.

You need to know some things pertaining to the messages you are sending and you also need to know how to use the signals you get to your advantage. You need to first know that displaying emotion is something that is more complicated than the frown or smile on your face. It has to do with the way you move the whole of your body.

If you want to convey success by using your body language, you can do it through the strategies mentioned below. The way you use your hands and the way you stand matter.

Your hands are capable of speaking for you, and sometimes, they can even do the speaking more than your mouth can. If you are experiencing difficulty establishing and expressing your confidence, you can try using non-verbal cues.

So, it is not a must that you must display complete determination with your body language every time. But these are postures and gestures that you should do your best to avoid. Mixed signals might be sent to an impressionable audience through these negative movements.

Has anybody ever told you that you look defensive or unfriendly whenever you cross your arms? This happens to be true. You need to be physically open as it can make people see that you are open-minded, happy, or confident. Paying attention to physical cues to know when a person is telling you lies is also helpful.

To portray emotional closeness and empathy, you need to mirror the individual you are having a conversation with.

Although smiling makes you appear more approachable and friendly, the different nature of showing your teeth has psychological effects. Ensure that you are not staring at the person you are communicating with awkwardly as eye contact is important.

Here are some ways you can start using body language to your advantage:

1. Using eye contact.

When you make eye contact with an individual, both at the time you are listening and speaking, it shows that you are fully present in the conversation you are having with the person. Many people have the desire to be heard, so when they believe that you are fully engaged with them, it creates a sense of comradery and warmness. Making eye contact with a person shows that you are not hiding anything.

Our eyes can also help us detect what people like. To do this, it is important that you look at the pupil size in combination with the direction in which a person is looking. Think about a recent visit you had to a restaurant. When you were deciding on what to eat, did you know straight away what you wanted to eat? Such decisions can be difficult. For instance, when making a choice between what food you should eat and what food you actually want to eat. One interesting thing is that when you have a difficult decision to make, your eyes will most likely move back and forth between the options for the food you are considering eating, and your last gaze is often at the option you finally go with. By paying attention to where an individual is looking, the options they consider can be known.

The eyes also have the ability to let us know if we experience an unpleasant thing. Therefore, if you want to find out whether a person is feeling good or bad, you can do this by considering the situation and their eyes as well.

Looking into someone's eyes can help you read their mind. How can you know what is going on in someone's mind? How can you get access to the information on their mind?
Many artists have used the phrase, "I can see it clearly in your eyes." Even if someone is trying to hide how they feel, they can't stop their eyes from telling the truth.

Looking at someone's eyes is a powerful thing, and it can help you read their mind. So how can you read someone's mind through their eyes?

If you want to know what is on someone's mind, you need to look deeply into their eyes and look for any changes that are occurring in their pupil size.

In addition to getting information from people, our eyes also send sensitive signals that other individuals can pick up on. You can determine emotions, such as anger and fear, just by looking at people's eyes. The eyes are also capable of revealing whether someone is telling the truth or telling lies.

Does this mean that individuals can read whatever is on someone's mind by looking at the person's eyes and that they need to look at only the signal from the eyes to get the required information?

There is no doubt that our "mind-reading abilities" are dependent on the context. You need to know that you might read the eyes of your loved ones better than the eyes of strangers because you can easily understand your loved one's facial expressions and know when they are surprised, angry, happy, and so on. Having evidence is important. It is the key that helps us make better assessments of the feelings of other people. But because individuals are unable to control how their pupil reacts, the eyes are an important source of information that is often under-used. They are capable of helping us develop better bonds with the people around us.

You might not be able to read someone's exact thoughts from just looking at the person's eyes. This ensures that the privacy of our thoughts is maintained. But eyes reveal to us much more than our assumptions tell us. Unlike our mouths, our eyes do not lie.

2. Stand straight and maintain a good posture.
While it is important to stand straight and maintain a good posture, this is important in your place of work. The reason is that it increases the power of your voice and also helps you appear confident. When you stand up straight, more air gets into your lungs as well as

through your abdomen, thereby maximizing your voice's sound and reinforcing your confidence.

3. Put your hand over your heart to emphasize a point.

Placing a hand over your heart to make a specific point is another hand gesture that creates a feeling of honesty and trustworthiness. This is the case because a lot of cultures believe this gesture is displayed by a person whose intentions appear to be genuine, or it is displayed by someone pledging allegiance or giving their word of honor. Listeners will likely feel more bonded and closer to you as a result of the subconscious idea that you are an open book, and they will also have a higher likelihood of trusting your intentions.

4. Gesture with an open hand.

When you are using hand gestures to convey a message, ensure that you avoid pointing with your finger. This is because when you point at other people, some cultures consider it rude and associate it with the allocation of blame. The person listening to you could feel like the object of criticism or feel accused, even if that is not what you mean. This can result in defensive and negative feelings that can get the point you are trying to make jeopardized. Instead, you can gesture with an open hand.

5. Subtly Mirror your listener's stance.

You don't have to copy every one of your listener's gestures. They will consider this creepy. But you can subtly mirror their speaking speed or stance as it will make them feel more accepted. Why is this so? Because, people tend to mirror the habits of the individuals that they like, and they do it subconsciously.

Although this information may appear to be a lot, you don't have to be an expert to benefit from nonverbal communication. You just need to know the body language basics and you will be able to avoid errors and interact well with people. Once you are confident in your skills and abilities, people will easily see your professional value.

CHAPTER FIVE:
Manipulation in the Workplace

You can identify dark personality traits in the workplace and communicate better with your colleagues.

You need to know the following:
- Manipulation in the workplace can happen when a colleague at work or supervisor uses coercion, shame, guilt, or other tactics to exploit another person on the team.
- If your company's CEO is a manipulator in the workplace, look for behavioral qualities and traits that show that your CEO might possess dark personality traits.
- Characteristics that can show that a person has manipulative tendencies include dark personality traits such as psychopathy, Machiavellianism, and narcissism.
- When you learn to spot dark personality traits, you will find it beneficial when it comes to understanding people and showing empathy professionally, especially when you have a manipulative boss in the workplace.
- Everyone has the ability to be manipulative but can decide not to act on it at work by staying mindful and being candid.
- When you are not sure of whether you are truly being manipulated by an individual at your workplace, it's helpful to check whether you are overthinking your interactions in the workplace.

It is as if you are having a nightmare: Imagine that you have a supervisor in the workplace who is hellbent on doing everything within their power to make life miserable for you, playing with your sanity and emotions. Perhaps this is a fantasy that can be tempting to believe on your worst days at work when you are sitting through meetings that are tedious or rushing to complete tasks to meet deadlines. Despite the hair-pulling and frustration that usually happens with jobs, you don't believe that any boss could be manipulative, right?

You need to understand that manipulation in the workplace is real whether it happens to you or you manipulate others. Even when you manipulate your colleagues at work and believe that you are doing it for the right reasons such as telling them they look good because you are trying to persuade them to help you do something, no real winner exists when you start playing puppeteer. You need to protect yourself against the professional world's string-pullers and learn to cope with manipulation that occurs in the workplace.

Workplace Manipulation Signs

If you are always voicing all of your thoughts at your place of work, you will get fired from work quickly. You need to understand that professional communication is required in work environments. That means preventing yourself from spreading or sharing unnecessary negativity, such as manipulative behavior, with your peers.

If your place of work is feeling hostile, uncomfortable, or tense, pay attention and watch out for the following signs that your manager or boss is a manipulative individual:

• Your manager or boss loves to point out areas where problems exist but they are never interested in doing anything to contribute to finding solutions to those problems: A boss who is manipulative might use your mistakes as a way to belittle you and insult your abilities instead of them to offer you helpful criticism or provide you with helpful idea. When you complete your tasks at work only because of anxiety, it is not healthy or sustainable. A good manager should point out the flaws you have or the areas that you need to improve upon, and they should also let you know ways that you and your colleagues can improve yourselves.

• Your manager or boss is using gaslighting or guilt to keep you motivated: For instance, asking you to take on extra work or staying late at work by convincing you that you are increasing their workload by refusing or that you don't work hard enough. And if your boss agrees to things such as deadlines or time-off requests but then changes their mind later, you need to also look out for similar tactics of gaslighting. When a person denies verbal abuse, it is a sign to pay attention to.

- It always feels difficult when having direct communication with your manager: Sometimes, communication in the workplace can be difficult. We can become tired, stressed, cranky, and so on. But you must ensure that you don't second guess yourself if you are constantly feeling as though your manager or boss is giving you the run-around. Manipulators are experts at withholding insights or details that might make you see their deceptive behavior.

Reasons for Workplace Manipulation

Manipulation in the workplace does not always happen on purpose. Even when it happens, it is not done with the intention of being malicious. Children quickly get to know which of their parents will likely say yes to them when they ask them for something. They also start paying attention to what causes their parents to say yes or no. Even as children grow older, there is not much difference in other social relationships. You may decide to flatter a colleague at work before asking them later to perform more tasks. Or, if the option is given to you, you may avoid scheduling your performance review at a time that is too early in the morning, before coffee brightens your manager's mood.

This is manipulation that happens in the workplace and it is the clean part of the manipulation. But tendencies of manipulation are linked to dark personality traits that every one of us shares.

We have seen that the main dark personality traits or the dark triad include:
- **Narcissism in the workplace:** Being preoccupied with one's

future plans, accomplishments, appearance, and self-obsession, is a symptom of a narcissistic personality. However, the individuals who display narcissistic tendencies are not always extroverts who are known to be masters at getting whatever they want. While these people's behaviors can be destructive, the individuals themselves should not be seen as demons. Like every other person, individuals with narcissistic personalities possess light and dark personality traits as well.

- **Machiavellianism in the workplace:** These individuals are usually very manipulative and during social situations, they have a chess player-like mentality. Machiavellians are not more interested in getting attention than narcissists: In their place of work, they are usually more focused on pursuing their goals. And sometimes, they can even do it with little regard for ethics or at the expense of others.

- **Non-empathetic tendencies:** Individuals who have psychopathic tendencies are characterized by emotional responses to stimuli that are blunted, and these individuals may not have a great ability to empathize with other people. As a result of this disconnection from others, psychopaths may behave impulsively, they may behave like Machiavellians, and they may also have little regard for individuals that their actions have affected.

Ensure that you discuss your situation with the HR department of the company if someone is continuously pulling your strings and the situation is getting out of hand, if you are being mistreated, or if you are feeling isolated. Like many other issues that are discriminatory, women and people of color have a higher risk of experiencing coercion or manipulation in the workplace.

While you will not have picture-perfect days every single day, it is important that the work environment is safe and free from manipulation.

Communication Strategies for the Workplace

Even if you want to manipulate your coworkers so that you can meet the goals of your team and harmonize with your colleagues, manipulation in the workplace can go wrong. If you believe that your coworkers need to be manipulated before you can get along with them in the workplace, you should pay attention to your strategy of communication or switch to a new category of work.

Instead of flattering your coworkers or using passive-aggressive workplace tactics that lack integrity, you can try doing the following:

Being more straightforward with your colleagues: The sense of fear or guilt that we have after making someone upset may make us try and manipulate or persuade the people we supervise or our coworkers when we need to ask them to do something for us. Be straightforward with them. If you want them to accept criticism, stay late at work, or take a look at an important project, ensure that you are open and respectful. Your colleagues will appreciate your truthfulness and honesty and this will allow you to provide answers truthfully and remove any unnecessary stress you may be going through from your day.

Evaluating your professional communication style's ethics: Are you the type who gives other people compliments to make them like you? Do you use guilt as a weapon to make your coworkers assist you? You may use these tactics that do not seem obvious because people usually rationalize their behavior when they are not sure of the right thing to do. While you may have a reason for manipulating your coworkers, it may result in unnecessary problems and harm in your workplace.

If you are not completely sure of whether your manager or boss is manipulating you, check whether you are overthinking the interactions you are having in the workplace. We usually spend considerable energy and time scrutinizing how we or other individuals interacted in conversations that we had previously, in work meetings, or at events. You may be suspecting a particular individual to be manipulating you but they may not be doing anything. Their strange behavior or comment may not be anything, or perhaps they may just be having a bad day. The beauty of professional boundaries is that everyone doesn't have to know. So, give other people space as they are human and need to be able to do what they want to do too.

Manipulation in the workplace is inevitable. Psychopathy, Machiavellianism, and narcissism are qualities that every one of us has and qualities that we may give in to occasionally. Not empathizing with people who are struggling with them as well as the temptation to display manipulative behaviors is hypocritical, even if the person is your manager or boss. However, nobody deserves to be manipulated and exploited in their workplace.

CHAPTER SIX:
Spotting Emotional Manipulation in Relationships

Emotional manipulation signs in relationships can sometimes go unnoticed as they can be very subtle. These signs have the ability to make you completely powerless. Manipulation is popular in relationships. Every one of us is capable of manipulating people.

However, when emotional manipulation continues to repeat, it can be a major red flag in relationships and can cause distress to the individual being emotionally manipulated.
How can you know when someone is going through emotional manipulation in a relationship?

Manipulation aims to alter the behavior of the person being manipulated. Every one of us has manipulated one person or the other at some point in our lives. For instance, when you convince your friend to go out with you to watch a movie and skip school on a particular day, that is manipulation at work.

You only tried to convince your friend to skip class and go watch a movie with you, and that doesn't appear to be particularly sinister, you may say. But when emotional manipulation continues to happen in a relationship, it can cause damage to the once-healthy relationship.

When individuals use mind games to try to gain control over you, they are labeled emotionally manipulative people. People usually use emotional manipulation to gain an unfair advantage over their partners or to control them.
It is important to remember that these individuals are not searching

for psychological tricks to manipulate others. This might even be unconsciously done, thereby making the manipulator need therapy to manage their issues.

Mutual trust, understanding, and respect are what a healthy relationship is based on.

You might find it hard to spot emotional manipulation as it can be subtle. It can make you feel helpless, misunderstood, and overwhelmed. We will take a look at the signs to look out for if you want to identify emotional manipulation in relationships.

How can emotional manipulation affect a relationship?

Emotional manipulation is capable of turning a relationship that is healthy into a sour one and it is capable of causing damage in the relationship. When wounds are created through emotional manipulation, it can get worse as time passes.

Emotional manipulation can affect your relationship in the following ways:
- It can lead to an increase in negative communication.
- It can result in low self-esteem.
- It can cause problems in communication as well as misunderstandings.
- It can create feelings of insecurity and a lack of trust.
- It can impact a person's sense of safety.

Emotional Manipulation Signs

Now, let us discuss some signs of emotional manipulation. We will be looking at emotional manipulation signs that are common in relationships. If you are having feelings of being manipulated in your relationship, you may be right.

They are always the victim.

The manipulator always acts like they are the victim who is innocent in the story they have twisted to suit them and paint you as the bad guy. You always believe that you are the one who made an error and feel like it is your fault that something is not working well. And you believe that the manipulator is the person who got affected by your mistake.

After some time, you start believing that the version of the story they have told is the correct one as your self-esteem decreases.

You always meet them at a location of their choice.

Have you noticed that you always meet the manipulator at a location of their choice?

It can be very empowering when you come to see them at their favorite restaurant or at their home. Although they feel comfortable and safe in an environment that is familiar, you are bound to be on edge. You get an unfair advantage from this, thereby causing a power imbalance.

You always feel misunderstood.

Do you always feel like they don't understand you? Feeling misunderstood is not something new in relationships. Emotional manipulators know how to make you believe the version of the story they are telling without you even realizing it. They thrive where there is chaos and always do things like pitching two people against each other while they watch happily.

If you notice that you are always in the middle of a misunderstanding, chances are that you are being manipulated.

Your weaknesses can be used as a weapon against you.

This is a key sign that a person is being emotionally manipulated in their relationship.

Suppose you always feel bad after opening up to this individual. Chances are, this person has been using your vulnerabilities and weaknesses as weapons against you and bringing them up whenever you are in the midst of an argument. This can be a huge problem for you.

You are the one being criticized.

No matter what you do, you always feel like you are not doing enough and your best will never be good enough for the manipulator. This is a key sign of emotional manipulation that happens in relationships.

You always get judged and criticized by the individual and this makes you start to lose faith in yourself and the desire to have a healthy relationship with people starts to fade. It is as if you are always being attacked for little things.

The manipulator makes you feel like they are the one doing you a favor

A person who is emotionally manipulative volunteers for responsibilities and tasks they have no intention to do and behaves as if they are actually doing you a favor by doing those tasks, only to bring it up during a misunderstanding and use it against you.

For instance, the manipulative individual might say they will make lunch every day only to bring it up later and say something like, "I always make lunch for you but you are ungrateful." They might take you on expensive vacations or buy you gifts and then bring it up later during a misunderstanding as a favor they have done for you.

All they see is the negatives.

Emotional manipulators find it hard to see the positives. They always see the negatives. For them, the glass is always half empty and not half full. They often have a pessimistic view of life and never cease to find faults in everything that you do.

These individuals have perfected the art of seeing negatives in a good situation.

For instance, if you are excited about a promotion that you received at work, the manipulator would quickly remind you of the additional responsibilities the new position requires instead of being happy about your promotion.

They never give you the chance to speak for yourself

Do you have a partner who never gives you the chance to answer questions for yourself but speaks for you even before you say a word?

One common sign associated with emotional manipulation in relationships is when you have a partner who never gives you the opportunity to share your opinion. The manipulator may invalidate your opinions when they talk to you.

When you are trying to make a point, an emotional manipulator may talk over you and interrupt what you are saying, thereby keeping you isolated from the ongoing conversation.

Aggression is channeled indirectly.

Passive aggressiveness is a common sign of emotional manipulation. What the manipulator does is to avoid confrontation with the person and then their aggression is channeled indirectly.

When they display inappropriate behavior, they are good at making excuses for their behavior and using silence as a means of punishment. Tools such as snide comments, microaggressions, and so on are also used to take you off balance while they are still being nice to you.

Insults might also be masked as compliments to get you confused. This is something that emotionally manipulative women usually do.

For instance, the manipulator may say something like, "You act so childish and immature sometimes, and it's cute." This confuses you and makes you wonder if they actually hate you or love you.

Ultimatums are a major part of your relationship.

Is your partner always dropping ultimatums?

You might have a partner who is quick to drop ultimatums and issue threats that they will leave you at every little issue. They don't mind making you feel insecure and anxious and love to have the upper hand in the relationship.

You may notice that you are constantly walking on eggshells whenever your partner is around and this is because of their behavior.

They make you doubt yourself and have feelings of insecurity.

Have you found yourself beginning to have feelings of security over things that you didn't even care about before?

This is something that happens when there is emotional manipulation in a relationship. Your partner may compare you to individuals they were attracted to in the past or their ex-lovers, they may complain about your weight, and ask you to be like another individual.

All of this makes you start having issues that were never present in your life. If this continues for a long time, you may find yourself having symptoms of mental health problems such as depression and anxiety.

They always belittle or mock you.

Do you have a partner that makes you feel like you are too small?

They may trigger your insecurities by passing snide remarks thereby making you feel insecure even when you are in the company of people.

They are not bothered about saying something like, "Don't listen to what she is saying; she doesn't know anything about being financially stable." She hates that I look at female models."

Spending time with these people always leaves you feeling drained.

They are always lying.
Have you ever found it hard to believe your partner because you felt that every word they say is a lie?

An emotional manipulator has mastered the art of lying about big things and small things. They are always lying about little things like what they ate for lunch and things that are more serious like whether they are still seeing their ex.

When an emotional manipulator is involved, you can never tell whether they are telling the truth, and this makes them angry.

You are always being blackmailed.
The manipulator can say something like, "Do this, or else…"
Emotionally manipulative people usually use blackmail as a weapon to make their victims do what they want them to do. They could issue threats that they will leak your private photos, expose you to your family and friends, and so on to put you back in line. The stress in the relationship may start making you feel like you are stuck in the relationship and have no way out.

You are facing too much pressure.
You feel like they are always monitoring and watching you and you always find yourself facing too much pressure. Living in a fishbowl is what some individuals call this. The manipulator pressures you into doing something you would not usually do. It can be something

like buying a property or car that you can't afford or getting butt or breast implants.

They use negative humor to highlight your weaknesses.
They use jokes and humor as a weapon against you and then when you get offended, they say you are over-sensitive. The jokes they crack about you are designed to trigger you and make you react. They enjoy making you lose balance, and you often find yourself wondering why they cracked a certain joke about you, whether it was a subtle attack on you, and what they meant by that.

Gaslighting is present in the relationship.
One of the popular examples of emotional manipulation is gaslighting. You are sure that a certain incident happened, but the manipulator insists that it didn't happen and you start questioning your sense of reality and sanity.

Your genuine issues and concerns are usually dismissed or minimized, and all of a sudden, you start believing the story the manipulator is telling about how the event played out.

They always enjoy causing a scene.
People who manipulate others emotionally are not afraid of dragging you into social situations that are uncomfortable for you. They love to yell at you, create a scene even in public places, or shame you in public.

This person even badmouths you to your families and friends while making them believe that they themselves are the victims. They may even come to your workplace. You usually dismiss your feelings because you don't want to create a scene.

You feel insignificant and never feel good enough.
You feel like you are insignificant and that you are never good enough for the individual. You also feel that nothing you do will

ever make you good enough for them. This person always makes you feel like the ugly duckling in your relationship, and you feel insignificant.

They always talk about your failures in the relationship and highlight them, and your successes are never celebrated.

You feel like your arguments and feelings don't make sense.

Emotionally manipulative people use statistics, research, and facts when arguing with you to prove their point. They are brilliant, thereby making you feel like you are fighting facts and statistics. And you may even start feeling like your arguments and feelings don't make any sense. You are being compelled by this tactic, and you begin to question your sanity when you are speaking with them.

Why Emotional Manipulation?

Most individuals pick up techniques of emotional manipulation from their dysfunctional families, so it is a common thing to see people consciously ask themselves the question of whether they are emotionally manipulative.

Many individuals may not even know that they are emotionally manipulative, as they do it unconsciously. Some people engage in emotional manipulation unintentionally.

The following is why individuals are emotionally manipulative:

- They don't have proper communication skills.
- Their self-esteem is low and they need to feel that they are powerful and in control.
- They don't have the social skills that are important for healthy interactions.
- Their emotionally manipulative behavior may be a result of a

disorder, such as narcissism, that they have.
- They grew up in dysfunctional families or broken homes.
- Their emotional wounds, immaturity, and pain.

How can you deal with the effects of emotional manipulation?

You need to first identify emotional manipulation before you can deal with it effectively. If you believe that your partner is unintentionally manipulating you, you can discuss the situation with them and ask them if they would like to go for therapy.

If you have a partner who keeps manipulating you despite all your efforts, you may need to rethink your relationship and get help professionally.

CHAPTER SEVEN:
Choosing Victims

There is a category of people who attract manipulators. We will look at those traits that attract manipulative people.

Emotional manipulators use dishonest tactics, guilt, and gaslighting to exploit the weaknesses that their partners have and maintain control of the relationship. So, what traits in an individual attract manipulative people?

If you are bothered about why you appear to have many manipulators in your life, you may want to know the exact traits you have or the things you do that draw them to you. You may also be wondering why you are attracted to people who manipulate you.

Why do you seem to be attracted to manipulative friends? First off, you are not the only one with manipulative friends. Many other people also have manipulative people in their lives.

If you notice that you are a magnet for manipulative people and constantly find yourself in relationships with manipulators, then one trait you may have is vulnerability. That may be one reason why you keep being a target for manipulators.

An emotional manipulator is a person who is an expert at influencing their partner's behaviors and feelings to their own advantage.

Manipulators usually use anger, guilt, gaslighting, button-pushing, and other dishonest tactics to exploit the weaknesses that their partners have and stay in control.

This pattern is quite common: individuals who are nice can

continually attract people who are manipulative, such as friends and partners, who abuse, exploit, and emotionally manipulate them. Why do nice people often get exploited and manipulated, and why do the same people seem to experience this over and over again?

Could something be wrong with these people?

• No, nothing is wrong with them, even though they continue to find themselves in relationships with people who are emotionally manipulative.
• Yes, they have specific traits that individuals who are manipulative find captivating. Their empathy and vulnerability make them targets for manipulators. They also want to help people and give people the benefit of the doubt.

These are wonderful qualities. However, the manipulator may also be seeing that you wear a label on your chest with a written message that says "Pick me."

You will soon learn to keep the manipulative individuals away if you learn to recognize the traits you have that draw them to you and work on the traits.

You can become vulnerable to emotional manipulation if you have these traits:

You lack boundaries or have damaged boundaries.
People who are manipulative are good at targeting individuals that have boundary issues. That means that there is room for a person who is emotionally manipulative to convince you that people who set boundaries are selfish people.

How does an emotionally manipulative person know that you have boundary problems? Individuals who have good boundaries often communicate their boundaries very clearly when they first meet you.

So, how can you fix this?

Set boundaries. Perhaps, setting boundaries is something important that you have to learn to do in life. You can say no and protect yourself when you set boundaries. Boundaries are important for every healthy relationship. So, ensure that you learn to set healthy boundaries and stand by them.

You love to take care of other individuals.

People who are empathetic love to do things for other individuals, and this is not a bad thing. But when healthy relationships are concerned, we care for individuals, not take care of individuals.

This may be shocking, but most individuals are capable of taking care of themselves even though they may not be experts at it.

Individuals who are emotionally manipulative are willing to play victim to make you give them your attention and take care of them.

So, how can you handle this?
You can fix this by allowing other individuals to take care of themselves. At first, it will not feel very comfortable, but when you notice that another adult has something they are struggling with, ensure that you give them the opportunity to work things out themselves.

Individuals who manipulate people emotionally love to play the victim. So, ignore that and use your energy to take care of yourself instead.

You are a believer in love at first sight.

Love at first sight looks good in the movies, but the reality is that love takes time. Someone may say they fell in love with someone immediately after the person said hello to them or right from the moment they met the person.

People who are emotionally manipulative like to target individuals with boundary issues. This means that the door is open for an individual who is an emotional manipulator to convince you that only individuals who are selfish have boundaries.

Remember, a person with low self-esteem is more prone to fall for an emotionally manipulative individual's deceit.

So, how can you handle this?
Love takes time to grow. It is developed with understanding, trust, time, and communication. If the person who is manipulating you emotionally is asking you to move in and live with him the same week you met him, you need to think twice.

Low self-esteem.

You may be telling yourself that everybody has low self-esteem at one time or the other. Although this may happen, this trait of low self-esteem is highly attractive to emotionally manipulative people when an individual has problems with self-love.

You choose a person who unconsciously makes you remember that you have parents who were dysfunctional. When you are not able to love yourself unconditionally, which means loving all the things that are easy to love as well as the things that are hard to love, you may attract to yourself a person who mirrors you.

It would help to know that emotionally manipulative individuals also lack unconditional self-love and have low self-esteem. So, what can be done about it?
You need to work on loving yourself.

Treat yourself the same way you would treat a person who is your best friend. If telling your best friend that he is horrible doesn't seem like a good idea then don't tell yourself that you are a horrible person.

And, of course, you can fake this until it becomes a part of you. You don't need to believe it at first.

You connect with people who are familiar to you.
Truth be told, no individual likes to feel awkward, uncomfortable, or different. You look for the road that is well-traveled, connecting with individuals who possess characteristics that you are familiar with.

Unfortunately, a lot of times, the familiar is dysfunctional. You may pick a person who unconsciously reminds you of your parents who are emotionally manipulative. If you are able to make the relationship you have with the dysfunctional partner work, you will be able to fix what was broken in you when you were a child.

You like this, right? Sorry, you can only fix problems that you have had from your childhood by working on yourself.

So, how can you fix this?
A therapist can help you out here. They will help you fix any issues you have that are unresolved so that you can stop attracting people who are emotionally manipulative. The traits we have discussed are the traits that make you more vulnerable and attractive to the manipulator.

Understand that being vulnerable is not a bad thing. You just need to ensure that you set healthy boundaries and do your best to protect yourself from individuals who are manipulative because the power to do this is in your hands.

CHAPTER EIGHT:
Mind Control

You can make your own idea someone else's idea. When you control someone's mind, you can put your idea into their mind and make it theirs.

This way, you get the person to do your work. People are not sure whether they should do that thing or not. But when you put the idea into their minds, they are able to do it.

You are aware that this will benefit you the most, but you act like it will only benefit other people. Making individuals worried about something is necessary. This happens in online shopping. A product is marketed online to the extent that you feel that you have to buy it at all costs.

Marketers also set a limit. They might say that there are only 50 products remaining, so it will make you move fast to buy them without thinking too much about the product. You will place the order quickly without any idea of how your experience with the product will be. When you do this, you are controlling the minds of people and convincing them to buy your product quickly.

You need to learn two things from this. First, you need to put your idea into the minds of the people and create a need for your product. Second, do not give them the opportunity to think about the decision or the opportunity to focus on any risks associated with the decision.

You can get people to tell you what you want to hear when your idea is already their idea.

Manipulators like to control other individuals just to prove that they are better than those individuals or to get their point of view across. Our thoughts are important and they are responsible for the actions we take. Check an individual's experience, as it will determine their future actions. We may not have complete control over other people's lives, but there are things we can do to get into their minds.

Try to improve yourself to get better instead of keeping other people down. You will feel better when you are improving your life than when you are trying to keep others down for your own advantage. Don't think of how to control someone's mind because you think they will perform better than you. This can also have a negative impact on you. For instance, a person who has an exam to write and is focused on controlling another person's mind because they think the person will perform better than them will only hurt themselves. This is because they will spend time focused on controlling the other person's mind to distract them instead of reading for the exam. This can create more problems for you.

Steps for Changing Someone's Mind

Is it possible to learn how to change an individual's mind? What techniques of communication work for this purpose? It can be hard to change a person's mind. This is because people often have their ways of doing things and it can be difficult to change the beliefs they hold on to. But good communication can help you with this. Talking to the person and knowing their thoughts can guide you on the right words to say and the right actions to take.

Do you really want to learn how to change an individual's mind? You can achieve what you want without bullying or forcing the person into changing their mind. This way, they will not resent you for making them change their mind.

You can do the following:
1. Start by appreciating them honestly and praising them.

- When someone is praised for the good things they have done, it is easier for them to listen to things that are not pleasant after they have been praised. If praise is not involved, it means the person is not being appreciated for the good things they have done and anything they are being told to do might appear critical.
- Offer sincere praise. For someone to sound genuine when they offer praise, they have to actually appreciate the person's work.
- The praise you give should not be formulaic. When formulaic praise is given, the person waits for the criticism that is coming.
- Be specific with the praise. Point out the particular things the person did well, instead of being generic and generalizing everything.
- If you are not happy with the work someone has done, you can let them know the areas they have done well in and the areas they should improve upon to perform better next time. This is an effective way to help someone improve. Sincere appreciation makes the person open to receiving your feedback and can be effective when it comes to getting an individual to change their mind and behavior.

2. Talk about the mistakes you have made before criticizing the other individual.

- When you admit that you have made mistakes, it shows that you are aware that the task is hard and that the mistakes that the person has made are understandable. This encourages the individual to rise to your level and makes their importance match yours.
- Have the genuine attitude that what makes you perform better is because of the more experience you have which translates to high personal standards that are currently above the capabilities of other individuals.
- This includes the relationship you have with children and entry-level employees. You should not expect a 12-year-old to make the same decisions that you make at age 40. You did not make the same decisions when you were 12.
- When you give unilateral feedback, it gives the impression of a person who is a perfect overlord chastising a follower who is flawed.

A person's importance is diminished.

Tactics for getting an individual to change their behavior

- "You may have made a mistake, but I have even made worse than you have made. No one was born with the knowledge of everything. Experience is what teaches us, and you are doing better than I was at your age."

3. Indirectly call attention to the mistakes individuals make

- When someone makes a mistake, avoid going all out to criticize them for it. You can indirectly call their attention to the mistake they have made. People are usually aware of what they have done wrong, so when you directly call their attention to it, it brings about resistance because it feels like you are issuing an order.
- When you approach someone's mistake indirectly, it gives them the opportunity to make their own conclusion. They are able to save face, thereby allowing them the opportunity to correct the mistakes they have made.

Tactics for changing an individual's mind.

- Offer sincere praise and then tell them how to improve without pointing accusatory fingers. You can say something like, you have done a great job working hard, and if you focus on adverts, you will increase the number of clients. Avoid saying something like, you have done a great job, but you did not bring in clients.
- This helps you avoid the negativity associated with the feelings of failure.
- If you notice that a person did not do a task well, do the task yourself and then show the work you have done to the person. A proper example of diligence is set by this.

4. Make the individual's fault appear easy to correct.

- This is an area that is important when it comes to learning how to change an individual's mind.

5. Allow the other individual to preserve their pride.

● People like to feel important. Since they have a craving for importance, if you take away their importance, they will resent you and it will be more difficult to influence them later. Allow people to preserve their pride, even during the times when you are giving them feedback.

● You can allow them to preserve what they care about and their pride.

● If you notice that a role doesn't match a person, focus on the other strengths that the person has and make those strengths shine.

● Accept that people make mistakes out of inexperience or momentary carelessness, and not that they lack the ability.

● Avoid embarrassing the individual who made the mistake publicly. Express confidence in the individual publicly, to preserve their social bonds.

● If you have to let people go, ensure that you express that you are not letting them go because of their work quality, but because the company's needs are changing. Tell them that the business believes in their potential and is rooting for them.

6. Give the individual a great reputation to live up to.

● Every one of us loves to feel important. When you are valued for your reputation or for certain traits, it makes you feel important, and you will work to keep feeling important.

● If you have the desire to improve a particular thing about an individual, behave as though the individual already has that trait as an outstanding characteristic that they have.

Tactics to use.

● If an individual has a poor reputation for the trait that you want an improvement for, it may sound disingenuous if you reverse it. Instead, what you should do is to praise a character trait the person has, and then link it to the person's reputation. For example, an individual may be a hard-working person but may always make mistakes. So, you can praise the individual's diligence, and let them know that they can overcome their carelessness and mistakes if they focus hard.

- You can say this to a customer who is angry: "I have always loved your patience and fairness, and I want you to apply those characteristics in this situation. Please forgive our customer service for their mistakes."
- To an individual who has rejected you: "I have respected you for your open-mindedness and I know you will be willing to reconsider our proposal and change your mind if presented with more information."
- Do this for individuals who have a history of being underappreciated: look for a good trait they have and emphasize it.

7. Instead of giving orders, ask questions.
- There are benefits that come with asking questions.
- It gives your partner the opportunity to make their own conclusions on their own. People usually like their own ideas more than the ideas of others.
- It preserves importance, agency, and pride. The individual is following their own orders instead of following another person's orders. This person has ownership in the path forward. Someone can be made to change their behavior this way.
- Your partner's creativity is stimulated. New ideas that are better might actually show up.

Tactics to use.
- "You might decide to consider this." "What are your thoughts about this?" "Do you think this would work out?"
- Ask your staff when you don't have a clear solution.

8. Praise every of their improvement.
- When you praise every improvement, the other individual is

inspired to continue improving.

- Don't say, "I'm not good at this. Whenever I praise someone, it stops them from achieving their full potential as praise gives them an early reward." When you declare your goals for your weight loss publicly, you already get some social recognition that you desire and this may make it self-defeating. But you should not let this stop you from praising people for their accomplishments.
- Individuals should know that people crave importance the way they crave food, and when you give them a little importance, it will increase their hunger for more.
- Look back on the events of your life and remember times when your entire future was turned around by a few words of praise. You can praise other individuals and make a positive impact on them.

Tactics to use.

- Some relationships, especially work relationships and relationships with parents, have changed into a cycle of yelling. You need to break out of this vicious cycle so that you can have healthy relationships.
- Praise should be specific. Instead of simply giving flattering remarks, pick out a particular accomplishment and praise the person for it. This way, your praise sounds more genuine, and it also forces you to look for genuine appreciation points.

CHAPTER NINE:
Persuasion: Getting People to Say Yes

One hard task for a lot of individuals is to get someone to say yes. It is not only salespeople that need this skill, we also need it. Knowing how to get a yes from your family, friends, clients, and boss is a skill u need to learn.

Although only a few individuals know how to make someone say yes to their offer, you can learn the right techniques to get any individual to say yes to your offer.

You can apply the techniques we will discuss in your day-to-day life and it can also be used when you have a service or product to sell.

Influencing with pre-suasion.

The act of influencing your customers' minds and getting them to have a soft spot for your product and be sympathetic about it even before you start talking to them about it is referred to as pre-suasion.

Your success is determined by the words you say right before you deliver the message that makes you successful.

You don't have to say anything. Your customers can even subliminally start falling in love with your product if you create an environment for that. For instance, a person who secured 4 jobs actually said something before the job interviewers started asking them any questions.

When the person asks the interviewers a question like, "What qualities or qualifications did you notice in my resume that made you select my resume?" the interviewers may start focusing on the person's positive qualities.

Here are two more scenarios where individuals said yes as a result of pre-suasion.

The first instance is when an individual went to different shopping malls to ask for the phone numbers of the girls who were passing by. He was not able to collect the phone numbers from the girls. However, he was very successful with getting the phone numbers of girls when he tried asking for their numbers close to a flower shop. In the case of the flower shop, it was successful because it got the girls in the mindset of romance.

In the second scenario, a company that sells furniture changed the background image in their adverts to test the adverts. They used the image of coins in one advert and displayed their furniture on clouds in another advert. People searched for cheap furniture on the company's website when they saw the advert with coins in the background. On the other hand, people who saw the advert with the clouds in the background searched for comfortable furniture when they got to the website of the company. An image is capable of influencing people's minds.

Instead of selling your products directly to the people, you subconsciously get the people to like your product first before you start selling to them.

Make them like you.

Studies have shown that people feel connected and have a high likelihood of saying yes to people they like. Look for common hobbies, similar values, and shared interests between you and the other individual, and use this tactic to get them to say yes. Spend time and look for genuine similarities that exist between you and the other individual.

Have a legitimate reason.

Having a reason for why you are making the request is important. It has to be a legitimate reason. Ensure that you use "because." Studies show that people are more likely to say yes to your request when you give them reasons for your request. People might even say yes to a request even if the reason is bizarre.

It is not enough to just give reasons; giving an incentive also helps if your request is very big. You can tell them that you would assist them in their future projects or you can give them a monetary incentive. Ensure that you know why you are making a request before you make it.

Show your knowledge and expertise.

Ensure that you always talk about your knowledge and expertise before you start telling them the main thing you want to say.

When people become aware that you are a person with a lot of knowledge and experience, they will carefully listen to what you have to say.

Talk about the books you have written, your awards, and your famous clients. If you have a product that you are selling, you can let the people know the number of years your company has been in existence and the number of satisfied customers your company has. This would increase your chances of getting yes. When you show your expertise, it brings about a dramatic change in the way the people you are talking to perceive your data.

Create scarcity for a sense of urgency.

When you have a product that is displaying a limited stock alert on your website, it can increase your sales. Your sales will be increased as a result of the fear of losing out on the exciting product. Prospects say yes when they have the fear of losing out on exciting opportunities.

Most individuals won't take any initiative unless they see that there is scarcity. The scarcity principle is used by sellers to increase their sales. Have you ever looked at products on an online store and noticed that it has a limited stock or a limited-time discount notification?

The notification creates a sense of urgency in the people's minds and they rush to purchase the products.

Let your audience know what is unique about your product and what is genuinely rare. You will find this same principle helpful and can use it in your day-to-day life.

For instance, if you tell your friend that you will only be free by this Saturday afternoon for the whole month, the likelihood of them joining you will be higher.

In the same way, you can let your colleague know that if they assist you with your project, they would gain new knowledge which would be a great addition to their portfolio. When you create scarcity, you will find it effective in helping you get a yes from people.

Social proof helps.

Social proof entails sharing testimonials of your product or service to build trust from prospects. Imagine going on a vacation in a country and visiting a new place where you have no idea of the best restaurants to go and eat at. If you find two restaurants, one with 2 people eating and another one full of people, which restaurant will you choose to eat at? I bet you will choose the restaurant that has many people, right? This is what happens when people are purchasing products or services online. They have a high likelihood of purchasing the product or service which has a rating of 5 stars.

A lot of times people make decisions without being aware of the right decision to make. During such times, they follow the decisions of others. In terms of sales and marketing, this is called social proof.

It involves making people see the social proof of individuals who look directly like your current prospect.

For instance, if you want to sell an online course to students, you can tell the stories of students whose income levels and age are similar to your prospects.

When you are trying to persuade other people to do something, the idea is to emphasize the fact that a lot of people are also doing that particular thing you want them to do.

Getting your foot in the door.

This technique is one of the most popular and most effective techniques.

For this technique, you first ask the person for something small before moving on to a bigger request. The small request you make should be something easy and something that many people can easily do. A lot of people use this foot-in-the-door technique. If someone wants to ask for money, they first ask for a small amount and then ask for a larger amount of money after some time.

When you are trying to make sales, you can request that your prospects sign up for a webinar or a questionnaire first then you can pitch the product after that. Ask them to do something small first that makes them committed and then you can later ask them for the bigger thing.

Label.

Labeling involves assigning a belief, attitude, or trait to an individual before making a request. Ensure that the request that you make is not inconsistent with the label. It should be consistent with it.

If you have a colleague at work who always submits projects late, some of your colleagues may be giving that colleague who is struggling to submit projects on time the wrong labels.

They might say something like, "he can never get any work done" or "he will always be late to submit projects." The individual will lose confidence and end up continuously delivering projects late when he hears his colleagues say such things about him. However, if you tell that colleague that they are dependable and hard-working, they will eventually start submitting projects on time.

Once your colleague submits the project at the right time, ensure that you give him compliments. You can say something like, "I have always known that you are a trustworthy and reliable person".

When you give them compliments, the compliments will motivate them to work harder and deliver on time, and they will do their best to always submit high-quality projects on time.

Sometimes, giving an individual a label is not necessary. Instead of giving them a label, you can encourage them to confirm that they possess desirable traits. This way, you are allowing them to self-label. Make it a habit of genuinely labeling people with the kind of traits that match the request you want to make.

The reciprocity principle.

The reciprocity principle is a social rule that shows people's willingness to give back to other people when they first receive something from them.

Can you remember the times when your friend or neighbor gave you a beautiful gift? In this kind of situation, there would be a feeling within to return the favor and give them a gift as well.

Companies may use this principle and give people free samples of their products in shopping malls. Studies show that when individuals use a free sample of a company's product, they have a high likelihood of purchasing the product. Reciprocity encourages giving. If you want to get other individuals to say yes to your request, doing something for them first will encourage them to say yes.

When you give someone something or do something for them with an element of personalization, they become obligated to say yes to your request. If you are looking for people to complete surveys, you can send the request with a handwritten message on a post with their name. Doing this will increase the number of people who will complete the surveys because you have taken your time to personalize the letter so it stands out. This encourages people to create time to respond.

Instead of looking for who can help you, get used to asking the question, "Who can I help today?"

Freedom to accept or reject the offer.

When you make a request, you tell the individual that they are free to either accept the offer you have made to them or to reject it. Many of us dislike it when a person forces us to do something. We want to have the freedom to make any decision we want to make and this is why you should let the other individual know that they can either accept or reject the request.

Make a plan for implementation.

Even if you persuade an individual to purchase your product online or perform a task, there is a low chance of them actually purchasing the product or performing the task. This is the case because making a promise is different from actually fulfilling it.

Social media has made many individuals procrastinators. So, you need to make a plan for implementation if you want to really commit to doing something. Making a to-do list will not magically make it happen. Commitment is necessary.

When individuals make a concrete plan without stating what task they will perform, when they will perform the task, and how they will perform it, the chances that they will complete the task are low.

Studies show that people usually act on plans when they make concrete plans. A plan that people implement usually has it broken into what, when, and how.

For instance, if you want to increase the exercise you do, you can state clearly that you will go for a run when you return home from work on Saturdays.

When you are trying to persuade other people, ensure that you encourage them to make a concrete plan on a piece of paper with clear details on how they will achieve the goal they want to achieve.

Give figures and facts and tell stories.

When you are persuading your audience, it is good to share the facts and figures with them. This is a helpful trick in sales. Stories can also be included in your pitch because stories often fascinate people.

Stories transport your prospects to another world. Even politicians are masters at using stories in their campaigns to get more votes from people. Motivational speakers and teachers capture their audience's attention through storytelling. Psychologists say that people get very critical of what they have been told when they are exposed to numbers.

The audience's ability to pick out inaccuracies in what has been presented is usually reduced when you tell a compelling story that connects with them. Remember that it is a human being who will use the product or service you are offering, so ensure that you use a warmer tone when talking to them.

Keep in mind that your product or service would be used by a human being. So, have a warmer tone when you speak to them.

Instead of always using numbers and charts to persuade your audience, ensure that you use pictures of real people. It is easy for people to form a connection with a subject when photos of real people are used.

Studies show that doctors would order more tests, conduct a more detailed analysis of the condition of a patient, and detect more abnormalities if the photograph of a patient was simply attached to a CT scan or an X-ray compared to when the patient's photograph wasn't attached.

This means that your chances of getting yes are increased when you humanize information.

Have a full understanding of the goal you want to achieve and then use a story to bring it to life. Look for characters that your audience can connect to and show their desires and motivation.

Give genuine compliments.

People often like to receive compliments from others. Humans are self-centered beings. Studies show that individuals have a high likelihood of responding favorably to the request of a co-worker if that co-worker complimented them right before making the request. There are many other studies that showed that when you give genuine compliments to people, it increases your chances of getting a yes from them.

Waiters are often given a bigger tip after giving diners compliments for the way they made a great selection of dishes from the menu.

In the same way, when hairstylists tell their clients that their new hairstyle is so beautiful, they get a bigger tip. Even though many individuals are aware that people often give compliments so that they can get others to do something for them, they still say yes to those people. It is good to give compliments, but you must ensure that you do not overdo it as it will appear fake. Compliments should not be generic.

Before asking anybody to get something done for you, think of something good that the person has done for you and then include a compliment when talking to them.

End your conversation on a high note.

Have you seen that singers don't usually perform the songs that are the most popular at the beginning or middle of their concerts, but at the end? Singers do this because they are aware that if they don't leave their most popular songs till the end of the concert, their fans will get excited and go home after watching the performance of the most popular song, thereby leaving the concert before it comes to an end. This doesn't mean that first impressions don't matter. First impressions start the conversation so they matter. But it is important that your conversation is ended on a high note. How an experience ends is usually more memorable and important than how it starts.

Do you remember you were having a wonderful presentation until your colleague poured a glass full of water on your laptop? You were having a memorable holiday trip until you had issues with your return flight that got canceled and you had to spend so much looking for a good hotel.

If you pay attention to ending your conversations on a high note and make subtle changes to make it happen, you will have increased chances of getting yes from people. Do your best to save the best news until the end. This way, people will feel the impact more.

So, you can use these strategies to effectively get a yes from individuals. Ensure that you understand your goal first before making a request. When making a request, give them the opportunity to accept or decline your offer, and don't be too pushy.

CHAPTER TEN:
Understanding Human Behavior

You need to understand the basics of human behavior to be able to read people's minds. Experiences help people relate well with the world. Your experiences may include replying to an email from work or even something that is as life-changing as giving birth to a child.

Whenever an individual has an interaction with an organization, that individual will have an experience. Whether that experience is transformative, mundane, or even something that is in-between, it will create an emotional response that, in turn, will shape the individual's attitudes as well as inform their future behaviors. Whether it is to stay late at work, recommend the business to friends, or buy more products.

So, there is a need for organizations to know how the experiences of people affect their feelings, thoughts, and actions toward their business if they have the desire to drive profitable behaviors. It is not enough to just recognize this connection. Organizations have a role to play when it comes to actively shaping how individuals process their experiences and how they respond to those experiences by managing the human experience cycle's five elements.

- The experience cycle: The things that actually happen to an individual during an interaction.
- The expectation cycle: What an individual expects will occur during an experience.
- The perception cycle: How the individual perceives their experience based on the expectations they have, which are evaluated against emotion, effort, and success.
- The attitude cycle: What sentiments and opinions a person holds

regarding the organization.

- The behavior cycle: How an individual interacts with a company, which is heavily influenced by the individual's attitudes.

Formation of Human Behaviors

Although it is important to manage the relationship between emotions, experiences, and actions to develop emotional bonds that are lasting, organizations should also have an understanding of why individuals have the feelings they have and why they do the things they do.

Although humans are quite complicated, this can be a tricky thing. People are not decision-makers who are completely rational and who only act on logic. Our behavior is also influenced by many other hidden factors. Organizations will struggle to consistently create experiences that are engaging if they fail to address these underlying determinants.

Fortunately, everybody shares some characteristics that are fundamental. When organizations recognize the traits that human beings have and embrace those traits, the organizations will be able to make connections that are lasting.

You need to know the following:
- There are two modes of decision-making that people have: the logical, slow, and deliberate one, and the one that is automatic, fast, and based on mental shortcuts and biases. People mainly use the latter one, which is also referred to as intuitive thinking, when it comes to making decisions, especially when they are in the midst of a crisis or stress. Unfortunately, instead of organizations to cater to people's intuitive side, many organizations spend a lot of time trying to appeal to people's rational side.
- People usually remember things according to the feelings the experience gave them, especially during the end of an interaction

and at the most extreme points. When designing experiences, think proactively about the emotions that will likely be generated by the experience during these critical junctures.

• Everybody sees the world through their own personal and unique lens. It is hard to put ourselves in another individual's shoes as a result of this reality. Leaders and employees are more familiar with the products, services, and processes of the company than their suppliers, prospects, and customers. A lack of empathy or miscommunications can be created by these knowledge gaps. You will be able to identify and mitigate resulting issues when you recognize this innate self-centeredness.

• People thrive on positivity and hope and respond well to feeling good about the future. Organizations that are effective motivate the individuals in their ecosystem, and they do this by painting a picture of success that will occur in the future that addresses their individual aspirations and needs.

• People like to form connections with other people who are like them. They usually trust those people that they believe are like them or those institutions that they believe are like them more than they trust others. Understand that the social groups that people belong to are an important area of influence, and look for ways to assist customers and employees in building connections that are meaningful.

• People have four intrinsic needs, such as a sense of purpose, progress, control, and competence, that they strive to fulfill. Instead of putting your focus on extrinsic needs such as price and monetary compensation, you can ensure that you are designing employee experiences and customer experiences that address these intrinsic needs.

There are many theories and definitions of human behavioral research, but generally, it is known as the study of how people interact with each other and how they interact with the environment around them. According to behavioral science, the human brain often relies on mental rules of thumb or heuristics to make satisfactory and swift decisions. However, these heuristics sometimes fail and result in cognitive biases, and they are systematic errors present in our thinking.

When organizations are creating experiences and managing them, they need to anticipate these heuristics and design around the biases and heuristics as they will impact people's behaviors, attitudes, and perceptions significantly.

While more than a hundred different heuristics and biases have been identified by behavioral research, they can be categorized into six:

- **The people around us influence us heavily.** This is about one of the six key traits that humans have. Humans are social creatures. As a result, individuals often go with the wisdom of people that they consider to be experts or they go with the wisdom of the crowd.
- **Individuals often prefer simplicity more than complexity.** Individuals often choose the options that they find easier to process mentally, even when an option that is more complicated is the better option. And it also applies to communications. People often like language that is simple and clear more than confusing buzzwords and corporate jargon.
- **Losses affect individuals more than gains.** The decisions we make are not based on the final outcome's rational evaluation, but the decisions are based on an unconscious evaluation of the potential losses and gains of each choice.
- **There is a misjudgment of our past and future experiences.** People often misjudge the past and future experiences that we have. Our memories are like a series of snapshots used to judge our experiences retroactively; they are not videos looping in our heads. We also struggle to make predictions that are accurate regarding future events or ourselves.
- **Individuals make decisions that are dependent on**

context. Decisions that individuals make are based on context, such as how a decision is framed, the unconscious priming effects that an individual encounters, the physical environment in which the individual makes a decision, or other available choices for comparison. Decisions that individuals make are not made in a vacuum.

• **The current emotional and visceral states of individuals affect their actions.** People's behaviors are influenced by how they are feeling during an experience. For instance, individuals act more impulsively when they are hungry. They rely more on intuitive thinking when they are experiencing emotions that are strong. Being aware of this can assist you in taking steps to defuse customers who are angry before requesting that they process a statement that is logical, such as a solution to their situation.

Organizations will be able to build stronger emotional ties with their audience, which will lead to higher profits and stronger loyalty when the organizations are able to create experiences that show how people actually think and behave instead of treating people like completely logical, rational thinkers.

Understanding the Behavior of Humans

Understanding the behavior of humans is many people's desire. There are individuals who love to look for typical patterns of behavior and also the common causes of destructive and unusual thinking and behavior. What makes human beings self-sabotage? What makes people commit suicide when it is not in line with our struggle for survival? It appears many people are only concerned about themselves so they take advantage of others to get what they want.

You need to know the following:
1. Many don't believe in themselves.
If everybody had more self-belief, this world would be filled with

less negativity and more positivity. No matter the self-doubt, people would grab opportunities, live their lives to the best of their abilities, and achieve more. When you make unfavorable comparisons to others, you believe that other people are better than you, and your self-belief decreases.

2. Everybody has a fear of something.
Every one of us fears something. It could be a fear of being alone or something like a phobia of spiders, which is an irrational fear. Fear promotes wasted opportunities. It paralyzes people. Often, the event is not as bad as the fear, but for those individuals who give in to the fear that they imagine, the fear stays in place.

3. Many people feel misunderstood.
Have you ever felt like you were standing on the outside and looking in? If you have, you are not alone. Many individuals have times when they feel misunderstood and alone. They have feelings of being somehow different from the billions of people that exist in the world. There will always be a person somewhere in the world who feels the same way as you do. This means that we are never really alone. Other people understand you more than you think they do. There is something universal that connects us all together, and this underlying universal understanding is something you may not be aware of.

4. Denial does not fix the problem.
People have learned different ways to justify their own behavior and fool themselves. Some people may physically abuse their partner and then justify it saying they don't understand how people cheat on their partners. Isn't it quite interesting to see someone justify physical violence but find deceit and lies in relationships appalling? There are individuals who tell themselves stories that are fake and that are not the reality yet this is done with the intention of coping with reality. Unfortunately, if you are thinking that denial fixes the problem; it doesn't. if you want to resolve anything, you need to first acknowledge the existence of that thing.

5. Our parents play a huge role in our success.

Our parents are important when it comes to the success we achieve later in our lives. Although we have total control over our lives as adults, our upbringing plays a crucial role in whether we become successful or not. It is important that we understand how our upbringing may help us or hinder us in life so that we can know what to do to get the most out of our lives. Many parents are not aware that they play a key role in the future of their children, emotionally, mentally, and spiritually.

6. Everybody wants to have peace of mind.

Everybody desires peace of mind but they don't know how to find peace of mind. You need to separate yourself from the noise of the world, avoid comparing yourself to others, and then find your own path if you want to have peace of mind. What do you desire to achieve while living here on earth? What do you consider important in your life, and are you having time to do what you consider important? When you allow too much external influence, your focus is diluted and you may lose your way and peace of mind.

CHAPTER ELEVEN:
Standing Your Ground

It is possible to deal with a manipulator and put them in their place. Ideally, a person will notice a manipulator and then run far away from them. But there are times when you cannot run away from them.

Sometimes, the person manipulating us is our colleague at work or our boss. Other times, the person is our adult child, spouse, or family member who uses manipulation tactics to get what they want from you and other members of the family.

Things become complicated. For these situations, some techniques exist that you can use to disarm the manipulative people in your life.

Here are the techniques:
1. Call the manipulator out.
One way to disarm a manipulative individual is to call them out. Let them know that you are aware of what they are doing.

If an individual is trying to bait you into an argument that you know you cannot win or if they are gaslighting you, you have the power to decide not to participate.

Here are some things you can say:
- "I am not going to discuss anything that is not relevant to this conversation."
- "We cannot talk if it won't be possible for us to honestly discuss this."
- "I think you are saying this to start an argument that will lead to a fight, so I am putting an end to this conversation."
- "You are asking for extra work that we didn't agree to from the

beginning. Why would I do the extra work?"

Once you say something like any of the above, it doesn't mean that the manipulator will suddenly leave you alone. It is unlikely that they would do that.

Manipulative individuals will fire up their tactics when they are faced with resistance, but that is what will make you know that you are taking back your power from them. Manipulators dislike it and will often lash out, but if you stand your ground. They won't be able to take advantage of you.

2. Reset the conversation.

One common tactic that manipulators use on their victims is to encroach on their personal space. When this person is having a conversation with you, they might move too close to you. They might try to give you a pat on the shoulder or back to make it more difficult for you to reject them.

When a person is trying to make you do something you don't want to do by using physical proximity, take a step back so that you can reset the conversation.

3. Maintain eye contact.

Manipulative individuals are good at asserting their dominance and getting what they desire by using eye contact. This is called the hypnotic gaze. It is when an individual focuses on you intensely, and it is designed to test boundaries.

Make them have a taste of their own medicine. This may require some practice, especially if the manipulative individual is aware of what to do to throw you off your game. You need to practice and master how to remain calm when a manipulator is trying to use eye contact to throw you off balance.

If you believe an individual is trying to use intimidation to manipulate you, say no to their request and ensure that you maintain steady eye contact in the process. If you want to put the manipulative person in their place, ensure that you make eye contact.

4. Respond with emotional neutrality.

Manipulative individuals are experts at weaponizing emotions for their own advantage. If they have a way to make you angry, ashamed, feel guilty, or get you worked up, they can use your vulnerability against you.

You need to remain neutral when dealing with the manipulator who continues to push your buttons. This is one way to disarm them.

This might require every ounce of strength, but you must ensure that you get the emotion completely out of your response and then leave instead of reacting in an emotionally explosive way.

- "I am not interested in following you to that place, so I am hanging up the phone."
- "I don't agree with what you think of me, and I will be leaving now."
- "I am sorry that you think this way. I am done with this conversation."

When you immediately take away access from this individual for as long as you need, this is when neutrality works best. That way, you will be able to take time to process everything and determine whether you want to proceed with this person or not.

5. Don't give manipulators an opportunity.

Refuse to give individuals an opportunity to make you their target for manipulation. If you have a colleague at work who likes to help you a little so that you can do something they want you to do for them, you can refuse to accept their help. You can say, "No thanks. I can manage on my own."

6. Boundaries are important.

You need to set boundaries, especially when dealing with people who are manipulative and whom you cannot easily separate yourself from, like your parents, grown children, coworkers, or siblings.

When we set boundaries, they protect us from individuals and things that affect our ability to work in healthy ways. The situation determines the kind of boundaries to set.

Here are some examples:

- You might refuse to talk about issues that always end in arguments.
- You might say that you will no longer lend money and put an end to conversations that have to do with finances.
- You might tell an individual that you won't respond to their text messages or answer their calls when you are at work or after a particular time of the day like 10 pm.

Be clear about the boundaries you have set and also be confident. When setting your ground rules, ensure that you use "I" statements instead of "you" statements.

"I won't be lending you money anymore. I am your friend, but not your bank."

The manipulator will resist, but as you stay consistent and firm, things will change. This does not mean that the manipulator will change, but it means that you will no longer be facing the same drama you used to face before.

7. Try the technique of fogging.

The technique of fogging is used in assertiveness training. You can use the tactic to deflate a situation and handle an individual who is aggressive toward you.

Look for the kernel of truth present in whatever the individual is saying to you, acknowledge it, and then after acknowledging it, move on from the conversation.

This way, you are able to address the parts that are true without engaging in the parts of the criticism against you that are not true or the exaggeration.

Fogging works this way:

Colleague: You failed to enter our office meeting into the time tracker.

You: Yes, you are right; I forgot.

Colleague: You don't always remember to do this, and it messes up our schedules.

You: I didn't remember today and I understand the impact it has on the tracking of our data.

Colleague: This is ridiculous. I should not have to ask you weekly for time tracking.

You: You had to ask me today, and I can see that it is frustrating.

When using the fogging technique, ensure that you stay emotionally detached and calm in the face of aggression.

This strategy is quite effective because you are not allowing yourself to be drawn into an argument or engaging with the exaggerated parts of the conversation.

The energy of the situation is deflated by this but you remain firmly rooted in the truth in this scenario. You never accept the parts that are not true.

For instance, in the scenario that we talked about above if it is only three out of ten times that you have forgotten to enter the tracking information, it means that your colleague is simply being hyperbolic.

Nobody says you should agree with things your colleague said that are not true, but what you can do is acknowledge the part that is true: which is that you forgot today.

8. Make the manipulator to be specific.

Manipulative individuals are masters at weaponizing generalizations. This can be something like pointing an accusatory finger at you that you are always doing damaging things to them.

Ask the person for examples, then after asking, turn it back on them. If a person accuses you of always doing something to them, ensure that you ask them to prove it.

"Can you give me some examples of some things that I have done so that we can fix the issue?" This might get them frustrated.

9. Everything should be documented.

This point is especially important in any situation that could have legal implications in the future or in professional settings. If you are aware that you are dealing with an individual who is manipulative, and who has a knack for gaslighting and dishonesty, then you need to document everything.

Write down everything that was said, when you had the conversations, and get everything documented. This is excellent if you need to have proof of their behavior, and you are also protected against the game of "who said what" that these manipulative individuals usually play.

10. Avoid getting isolated.

Manipulative individuals do their best to keep you dependent on them professionally, financially, emotionally, romantically, or any combination of these. They do this by isolating you from your family and friends.

Knowing that you are not spending enough time with your loved ones and close friends is the first step to take towards breaking free from the grip that a manipulator has over you.

11. Don't give the manipulator what they want.

Individuals who are abusive often feed off negative emotions and they also know exactly what to do to push buttons to get a response from their victims. When you see this coming, don't take part in it.

If you know that a call from a family member will be filled with lies or drama, you can ignore the call.

If they continue to call and you make up your mind to speak to them, don't give room for things to turn toxic. You have the power to tell a person, "I am not going to do this particular thing, and I won't change my mind about it."

12. Use calm persistence.

This technique is a skill that is also known as "calm persistence." You continue repeating your main point or saying what you want over and over without raising your voice tone or getting angry.

It involves unwavering and staying calm in the face of manipulation. You stand by your message and refuse to become pulled into an argument or a conversation that is sidetracked.

Suppose you are planning an outing with a friend who is attempting to pressure you into spending a large amount of money on a more expensive option.

Your friend: "We should spend the entire time at the Resort. We will have a great experience."
You: "I would prefer we go to a place within our budget."
Your friend: "But give it a second thought. The amenities and the beautiful views. We should not miss this once-in-a-lifetime opportunity."
You: "It looks great, but I would prefer we go to a place within our

budget."

Your friend: "You are always playing it safe. Won't you like to make some beautiful memories?"

You: "I understand what you are saying, but I would prefer we go to a place within our budget."

Your friend: "I will make up for the difference. Let us enjoy the best and you can pay me back much later."

You: "I appreciate the nice offer you made, but I would prefer we go to a place within our budget."

In the scenario above, the friend who is hypothetical is trying different ways to make you accept choosing the more expensive option. When you continue to repeat your main point and you keep saying that you want to stay within your budget, your friend will eventually get the point and stop asking.

Manipulation involves control and power. You will be happier when you are able to take back your power and control of your life from the manipulator. Although we have discussed helpful strategies, it is important that you also get support when needed.

It is not your fault that you are being manipulated. Don't consider yourself a weak individual if you find it difficult to employ some of these tactics, especially if you are using the strategies against loved ones.

If you find yourself feeling trapped in a manipulative relationship, see a professional for counseling or help. A trained therapist can guide you and help you with strategies that are specific to your situation.

CONCLUSION

Do you have a partner that creates unreasonable rules that you must follow? If they set impossible deadlines that you must meet, if your bathroom breaks and mealtimes are strictly regulated, and you have no access to your friends or your own money, then you are being manipulated.

When your partner, who is the manipulator, is doing all they can to make you follow a strict set of rules by taking all your decisions away from you, it can be frustrating. This prevents you from thinking for yourself, and when you are not thinking for yourself, it becomes easier for the manipulator to implant their own agenda.

You may have been putting up with this for a long time, but this does not have to go on forever. You can prevent people from controlling your mind. If you notice that someone is manipulating you, you have to break free from their grip and their attempts to manipulate you.

We have talked about the steps you can take in this book. If you want to break free from the manipulator's grip, you need to follow what we have discussed.

Remember to remain in close contact with your family and friends because a manipulator can isolate you from your family and friends so that they can have total control over you. They might take you to their own location where they have all the power. Refuse to allow the manipulator to stop you from seeing any of your family members or friends. If they insist on preventing you from seeing your family members and friends, don't listen to them. You must insist on seeing your family members and friends. And if the manipulator still says no, you can walk away.

Refuse to put up with the manipulator's sulky or moody behavior. Treat that behavior with disdain, and don't fail to tell them that the behavior is childish and immature and you won't put up with such behavior.

You can tell what a person is thinking by checking for their pain points, and you can do this by asking them the right questions. You need to establish a personal bond with someone to be able to know what they consider valuable.

When having a conversation with someone, you have to be a good listener and not someone who talks more than you listen. You can't be talking non-stop without really paying attention to understand what the other individual is saying. That is not how to have a conversation. Poor communication is something that affects relationships a lot, and a manipulator might be a poor communicator. So, you need to work on having effective communication with them.

Sometimes, you will want to know what is on someone's mind before you say anything to them. This can help you say the right words and do the right thing. Saying the right words can help you close business deals and develop relationships that can last for a long time. If you want to know what is on someone's mind, you need to study their body language and follow the steps we have discussed in this book.

What triggers an individual's emotions? Where is the individual's comfort zone?

You need to give the person a chance to speak. Don't be the only one speaking non-stop. If you want to form a connection or get people to take action and purchase your products or services, you can do it. Ask questions that are open-ended questions that give the individual the chance to share their challenges and strengths. You can also share stories about the things you have done for other people. People will often acknowledge if they have the same issue when you share your story with them, and this can help you better understand their needs.

It can help to consider personalities. Observe the qualities an individual has to determine what they consider important and who they are as a person.

Someone may be very analytical and relate well with people when they come prepared and methodically lay out their ideas. They may prefer that people be prepared to use numbers to back up their initiative. And if a person comes to them but doesn't do that, then the person may lose the opportunity to win them over.

You can search for clues into a person's personality by paying attention to verbiage and characteristics. An individual who likes to be dominant, for instance, might have a handshake that is overly firm. Sarcasm will often be inserted into a conversation by individuals who welcome humor. You can determine their approach and their values by using these clues.

Nonverbal communication helps with mind reading. Don't forget to pay attention to body language clues as nonverbal behavior is important.

If a person leans in, it means they are engaged in the conversation. If they turn away, look down, or back up, it means that they are not relating to whatever you are telling them.

You can also get clues from a person's tone of voice. For instance, if a person is responding to you in monotone, it means that they are most likely not interested in what you are saying and they are not attached to your concept. If the person looks at you and moves closer to you when you speak, it means that they are finding what you are saying valuable.

We have said that you should pay attention and be a good listener. Ensure that you listen to what a person is saying, and also listen to what the person is not saying. While this is more difficult when the conversation takes place over the phone, a voice that is passionate or engaged is obvious and cannot be hidden. It also shows when a person is frustrated.

You will hear a sigh or the person's tone will change. Developing a good ear that has the ability to listen for subtle sounds is important.

Avoid communicating by email anything that involves emotion or that is critical. You can make a phone call instead. Emails can make it hard to be perceptive and they are hard in conveying what the words mean.

The ability to change the mind of an individual when they already have their ways of doing things is an elusive skill. You may find it frustrating when you are unable to convince someone to see things from your point of view. Even when you are sure that what you are doing is the right thing.

A lot of the things we do to change an individual's mind do not work as well as intended. Many of us have received training on the wrong ways to influence people. This is what makes us have little success when it comes to persuading people. New studies in behavioral sciences tell us what makes the old ways futile.

We need to put an end to using our gut instincts to change the minds and attitudes of people, including their logic, reasoning, and aggressive selling because they usually don't work. We need to use a different approach.

But things get easier and clearer once you understand how individuals make their decisions. You will see a positive and noticeable change in how your suggestions are viewed by people.

You will discover a surprising willingness and less resistance and they will say yes to you.

It can be hard to change a person's mind. Studies show that people argue with us more when we reason with them. Our efforts are spent on people's rational minds and this makes them resist us and argue with us more.

The good thing is that there is now an easy and reliable way to change the minds of people. A complicated approach is not needed to convince people to accept your view of something. You can win people over through some easy solutions that help to align their subconscious minds with you.

You can change someone's subconscious mind. It will initially be hard to focus on people's emotions. Our instincts make us give reasons for the choice or option we bring. This will hurt your chances at changing the minds of people so it is important that you suppress this urge.

You will engage someone's conscious mind if you rationalize with the person. And their conscious mind is not in charge of their decision-making. When you get a person subconsciously aligned with you, it will be easier to get them to do what you want them to do. They will easily say yes to you if you do this well. When you give the person reasons why they should listen to you and do what you ask them to do, the person will be moved to change their mind and be in agreement with you. Mastering the art of human psychology is not something unattainable. You can achieve it with practice and it will help you to become more successful in life.

Made in the USA
Las Vegas, NV
01 April 2024

88100746R00066